Writing Kidlit 101:

A Self-Guided Course

Writing Kidlit 101:
A Self-Guided Course

Victoria J. Coe

Cheryl Lawton Malone

Write On Productions

Boston

Write On Productions, LLC, Boston, MA

First published in the United States by Write On Productions, 2023

THE LIBRARY OF CONGRESS HAS CATALOGUED THIS EDITION AS FOLLOWS:
Coe, Victoria J. and Malone, Cheryl Lawton
p. cm.
Summary: "A self-guided, workbook-style course designed to teach the craft of writing children's and young adult fiction." – Provided by the publisher.
ISBN 9798987666548
[Creative writing – Juvenile fiction.]
I. Title
LCCN 2023933784
[Non Fic] – 808.068

Dedication

To our husbands

with love.

—VJC & CLM

Contents

Hey there!

Welcome to Writing Kidlit 101! We're thrilled that you're here.

Maybe you've always had stories in your heart. Maybe writing is a recent obsession. Wherever you are on your journey, whatever your WHY, you're obviously committed. You showed up.

That's a big step!

We created this course for you. You're busy. You're juggling life. You don't have the luxury of attending a class in person — or even online. You need flexibility. We hear you, we've been there, and we've got you.

As experienced authors and teachers, we firmly believe that an understanding of craft combined with a grasp of the market and a process that works for you is the best way to unlock your potential.

That's the secret sauce of this book.

Our goal is to give you the tools to write the story that's in your heart AND that kids and teens want to read.

And just so we're on the same page (see what we did there?), we are not going to teach you the "right" way to write. That doesn't exist. Sure, there are rules. But rules were made to be broken.

We promise to educate you, ground you, and familiarize you with best practices and the realities of the market. So if you do choose to go rogue on something, you do it consciously, with authority, and for your own great reasons.

Okay, Let's Back Up a Sec

This course will explore the 3 main categories of kidlit. Think: picture books, middle grade novels, and young adult novels. We will not cover any subcategories — so no board books, easy readers, early chapter books, rhyming picture books, verse novels, upper middle grade, short stories, poetry, nonfiction, comics, or graphic novels. We simply don't have the space, though you can certainly apply what you learn here to those categories if it feels right.

Now when we said we've been there, we weren't kidding. Both of us dreamed of writing kidlit while multitasking our way through careers and kids. For years. Decades, even. Our dreams turned into reality because we didn't stop learning or trying. We had plenty of reasons to give up. We just didn't.

Passing it On

Being teachers, paying it forward seemed only natural. We've each taught hundreds of students like you — people with an itch to write and a hunger to learn. This book is a mash-up of our real-life classes, the ones we designed for college and continuing ed students. The content is inspired by our own education in the field and our personal experience as acclaimed children's authors. We couldn't be prouder that some of our former students have gone on to become hugely successful and award-winning kidlit authors. Go, them!

We believe — scratch that — we KNOW — that if you arm yourself with the right info, unleash your own unique creativity, and put in the work, the sky's the limit. It's really that simple. And that hard.

The following 10 sessions are a self-paced course to get YOU to the next level — whatever that is for you. The sessions build from nerdy stuff to big picture while hitting everything in between, plus tips and tricks, practical writing exercises, extra credit, and assignments that we've titled "Calls to Action."

And here's your first call — carve out some alone time to work on each session. Set up calendar alerts. Or team up with a friend. Hey, invite a group of friends to go through the course with you!

Get a notebook — a dollar store notebook, a fancy notebook (your call) — and use it to take notes, jot down ideas, and make lists as you go. Do what's right for you. Take the sessions in order. Skip around. Go back and do everything twice.

Honor your process. Soak it up. Soak it in. Get everything you need. And don't stop until you do.

Our Stories

Before we get to it, you're probably wondering about us and OUR WHYs. So here you go.

Victoria:

Deep down, I'm a Jack Russell terrier. Once I decide to go for something, nothing will stop me. I got the bug to write for children as a mom reading every night to my own kids.

For the next 15 years, I read every book, took every class, joined every group, attended every conference, and wrote my little tail off. As a marketing professional, I was into the querying game. But after coming thisclose way too many times, I decided to really go for it. I hired a top kidlit editor, Deborah Brodie, to design and coach me through a personal MFA program.

A few years later and after Deborah tragically passed away, I landed my dream agent who sold my first of many books, *Fenway and Hattie* (Putnam/Penguin Young Readers, 2016). Excited to give back, I created a kidlit curriculum and taught at the Cambridge Center in Harvard Square for 3 years — a job that I completely threw myself into and would still be doing if my travel schedule allowed.

Along this journey, I've made countless amazing friends and honestly feel I could not do what I do without. The very top of that list is Cheryl, my brilliant critique partner of more than 10 years. Writing this book together is truly an honor and a dream come true. Whether or not you're a JRT like me, I urge you to dig in and see where your creativity can take you.

Cheryl:

Victoria came up with the idea of writing this book and I thought it was brilliant. We've been critique partners for more than a decade. After years of hard work, we landed agents and publishers. We both taught kidlit writing courses. Why not pay it forward by making the material accessible to a wider audience? Add to that the fact that we share an incredibly nerdy love of craft and learning. Well, my answer was an instant YES.

On an emotional level, I also want you to know there is no expiry date for dreams. After 25 years as a biotech attorney, I took leave to get a Master of Fine Arts at Lesley University, Cambridge, MA in Writing for Young People. Anxious to jump into my new career, I accepted a position as an adjunct professor at Lesley teaching Writing Children's Literature.

Since the publication of my first two picture books, the award-winning *Dario and the Whale* (Albert Whitman, 2016) and *Elephants Walk Together*, (Albert Whitman, 2017), I've expanded into lecturing and manuscript consultations. But mostly, I'm excited to share this course with you because writing for kids is worth every nervous submission, every rejection, and every hard-won, thought-out word. Simply put, writing for kids is magical.

- Session 1-
What is Kidlit?

The Marketplace

*K*idlit is short for literature published for toddlers, kids, and teens. Publishers, bookstores, and libraries divide kidlit into 3 main categories — picture books, middle grade, and young adult.

Books published in each category are meant for a specific age group with its own unique wants and interests. Now, more than any other time in history, the kidlit that's flying off shelves — and ultimately into readers' hands — speaks directly to today's kids and the issues they face and wonder about.

Let's Start with the Littles

Picture books (PBs) are illustrated stories for children ages 2 and up, intended to be read aloud — Think: strong emphasis on word play, meter, rhyme, alliteration, and repetition. Typically, the story is narrated by a child or animal main character that will draw in a young audience.

Today's picture books are short — 500 words or less — highly engaging, and brilliantly illustrated. The text and pictures are meant to be experienced together. Neither should tell the whole story.

Take a look at the bestseller lists and you'll see groundbreaking stories that go above and beyond what you probably remember as a kid. It's no longer enough for a picture book to be cute or fun or interesting. Today's standouts are full of original ideas, non-traditional ways of storytelling, and inventive formats. Check them out. They're all over the place.

But there's one important way that the picture books of today and those from a generation (or two) ago are still the same. Serious, funny, mindful, or whimsical, the great ones are read over and over. Again and again.

Meeting in the Middle

Middle grade (MG) novels are written for kids aged 8–12 who can read on their own or listen to the books read aloud at home or in school. Word counts usually range from 25,000 to 50,000 — though fantasy can go higher. MG is typically not illustrated, as kids in this age group like their books to feel "more grown up."

MG readers love to peek into the lives of kids a bit older than they are, so the main characters tend to be 11 or 12, unless they're animals. Publishers are also starting to realize the need for "upper MG" — story topics on point for 11-12-year-olds, but with main characters as old as 13-15.

Speaking of story topics, MG features classic themes like friendship, navigating family and social situations (bullies and first crushes), self-discovery/growing up, grief, courage, humor, and adventure. But today's MG pushes boundaries, too. Topics like abuse, addiction, mental health, social justice, immigration, identity — you get the idea — are all fair game.

Regardless of topic, whether the book is serious or funny or somewhere in between, the kid main character is the star who saves the day. They're the one who triumphs at the end. Adult characters can help. They can be cheering squads or mentors. But they can't steal the kid's thunder.

Even though they're shorter and less mature than YA novels, MGs still tell rich stories with subplots, and leave the reader with a happy — or at least hopeful — ending.

Sitting at the Big Kids' Table

For fiction aimed at teens — Young Adult (YA) novels — anything goes. That means yes to sex, drugs, crime, explicit language, you name it. Word counts range from 40,000 to 80,000 with multiple subplots and fully-developed secondary characters.

YA main characters are almost always 16–18. They can drive (or have friends who can) and attend high school, not college. They don't own homes, pay rent, or have full-time careers — though summer or part-time jobs are great.

Of course, if they live in a fantasy world or a challenging real-world environment, they can support their parents, be an apprentice or next-in-line to the throne. They can even be completely on their own.

The point is, even in fantasy, YA main characters are not adults. No matter what kind of world they inhabit, they're not "of age." They're not totally empowered. They can handle responsibility — or think they can — but they're not fully mature. Whether they're focused on their future or struggling to survive, they're not living the kinds of lives we expect from (even poorly-functioning) adults.

Oh, and lest we forget — YA characters always get into trouble (or maybe we didn't have to say that).

YA or Adult - What's the Difference?

Two things — the age of the main character and the teen perspective. THE END. Seriously, it's just those two.

But maybe we shouldn't have used the word "just." The teen perspective is everything in YA.

YA readers care about teens and teen issues. Full stop. If the main character's mother has cancer or loses her job or is an addict, they might feel sad or helpless or angry. But their biggest concern is how this new reality will affect THEM. How are THEY dealing with their sadness? How are THEY navigating feelings of helplessness?

What are THEY going to do? YA readers don't want to read a subplot told from Mom's POV, how she's dealing with those same issues. Get it?

What's Trending?

So how do you find out what's being published today? Or better yet, what types of books are editors buying that won't hit the market for a year — or 2 or 3 — from now?

A couple of ways. Visit an independent bookstore — if you're lucky enough to have one nearby — and talk to the booksellers. Ask them what's new and hot in your category — particularly from debut authors. Those are the ones who broke through the noise and competition and sold their story without a big name or rabid fans — just like you want to do. (Pro tip: Do the same thing at the library by talking to librarians.)

Subscribe to Children's Bookshelf from Publisher's Weekly (Google it). It's free! Search online for debut authors' groups for next year, the current year, or last year. Make sure the group includes your category (they're all different). Scan the books on their sites or blogs. Follow their socials.

Create a free account on e-galley sites like NetGalley and Edelweiss. Request e-galleys (advance copies of pre-published books) that grab you. There's no guarantee you'll get approved, but if you do, you can read pre-published books for free. It's well worth a shot.

Regardless of how, make sure to get a feel for what's hot in your category.

Please, No Robot Fairies!

Now, once you know the latest trends, please don't follow them! If robot fairies are all the rage, every editor's inbox will be stuffed with robot fairy books. You want to stand out. Knowing the trends means you're informed. It doesn't mean you're a sheep.

Also, don't forget — times change. What was popular or (gasp!) cool when you were a kid is history. Sorry. Band-Aid is off. Not only will your story have to compete with other books, but also with video games, streaming platforms, social media, and who-knows-what for a kid's attention. Books from the past are horrible mentor texts for today's smoking hot new releases.

Write the story of your heart. That's the story that will be authentic. That's your secret to success.

> Okay, let's get nerdy about categories and genres real quick.
>
> CATEGORY means WHO the book is for — PB, MG, or YA.
>
> GENRE — humor, mystery, fantasy, coming of age, historical, contemporary, romance, adventure, and so on — refers to WHAT type of story it is.
>
> That's it!

Tips and Tricks

- Choose the age of your main character wisely. Up to 6-years-old means your story is a picture book. 8–12 places your story squarely in middle grade. But remember, 12-year-olds rarely like to read about 8 or 10-year-olds. So if your main character is 8, you might have a great story, but no audience. A main character who is 16–18 needs a clear teen voice and real teen issues, no matter what the setting.

- Remember, your main character must solve the story problem. Help is okay. Grandpa jumping to the rescue? NO.

- Think about where your story fits into the market. What books are comparable to yours? Find books written in your category and genre in the last 3 years. Forget about using *Harry Potter* or *Twilight* as comps. They are old by kidlit standards.

- For picture books, do not — repeat, do not — be your own illustrator or have your children illustrate your story UNLESS you or they are professional illustrators with portfolios full of amazing expert illustrations. If you ARE an author-illustrator, go for it! If not, write your best story. When your text is lucky enough to secure an agent, appeal to an editor, and make it through an acquisitions committee, the publisher's art director will match you with the perfect artist who will take your story to the next level.

- As you're researching, you can quickly find the word count of almost any kidlit book by searching for it at arbookfind.com.

Writing Exercise #1

Go back and reread 5 of your fave kidlit stories. List the age of the main character in each. Note how the authors convey the narrator's child-like (or teen) perspective. Compare those books to your fave adult read. What besides word choice is different?

Writing Exercise #2

Come up with ways that each of these ideas COULD be developed into books in each of the 3 categories — PB, MG, and YA. Remember to focus on the age of your main character and their perspective.

> A book about a refugee family.
> A book where the main character navigates a summer away from their loved ones.
> A story about a dog.
> A book written entirely in text messages.
> A classic "hero's journey" story.

Writing Exercise #3

Pick 3 of your fave kidlit reads from way-back-when. Jot down reasons they might not get published as new books today.

Writing Exercise #4

Take a picture book published 30+ years ago and put it side by side with a PB published within the past year. List all the differences.

Writing Exercise #5

Think about an incident that happened recently — you lost your bag, you were late, your best friend won an award. Now invent a main character who is 4-6-years-old (PB), 8-12-years-old (MG), or 16-18-years-old (YA) and write a paragraph describing the event as if it happened to them. If you're just starting your kidlit journey, take the time to write the paragraph from all 3 age groups. If you're drawn to one, start there.

Extra Credit #1

Think about your fave adult character. In your notebook, journal/brainstorm what they might've looked like and acted like as a child. Note the age of the character you invent — this might be your sweet spot.

Extra Credit #2

Think up 3 ideas for potential MG or YA novels that no one would have dared to publish when you were a kid.

Call to Action

Browse the shelves of your local library or bookstore for the kidlit category you want to write. Jot down any thoughts, questions, and observations in your notebook about the types of books you find. Read the top 5 new-to-market titles (pub date within the last 3 years) that the staff recommends in your favorite genres.

- Session 2 -

Hello, My Name is . . .

Character

Kidlit readers like stories with intriguing, exciting, or dramatic plots. But what they really fall in love with are characters.

Not just any characters. Compelling characters they can relate to and root for. Characters with lives that mirror their own or characters totally unlike them that they might be curious about. Even characters they never even knew existed.

The point is, readers can't wait to see what their favorite characters will do next, how they'll react, and whether they'll live happily ever after. Or not.

> If you want the reader to care about your story,
> the reader needs to care about your character.

Great characters come from two places — your imagination and your heart. Not either or. Both and.

Here's why. Fiction is fiction. It's not exactly the same as real life — otherwise it would be nonfiction, right? Meaningful fiction gives readers insight into real life. It reveals something about life that they can connect with, that stirs feelings, that inspires them. This is true of all kidlit, whether it's picture books, fiction for 8-year-olds, or fantasy for teens.

The stories kids read become a part of their lives. They expand their worldview. They matter.

Sure, you can write kidlit without emotion, without depth. Plain old silly stories exist. Remember — rules can be broken. Break them for your own reasons, then go for it.

Just know that we — and most kidlit readers — are fans of stories with heart. And here are two ways to create them.

Time to Shape Up

The first way is to start with your imagination. Wow us with characters who are unique and fresh. As a creator, you have the ultimate power and freedom to give them any set of traits, any kind of background or backstory, and any kind of life you want them to have.

Try lots of ideas – the first kid to go to Venus, a high school junior who's memorized the dictionary, a rabbit with a freakishly long tail. Have fun. Don't feel you have to nail your characters on the first try.

Think about things like names. Move on to demographic info like gender, age, race, ability, and whatever else seems important to you. Consider what kind of life they live – place, family, status, friends, social setting, anything else that might impact them. Brainstorm. Make lists. Move ideas around like puzzle pieces.

Play dress-up — try on different personality traits, strengths, weaknesses, passions, goals, and motivations. Think about questions like these:

> What makes the character who they are?
> What gets them excited?
> What do they care about?
> What do they hate?
> What scares them?
> What do they look like?
> What do they like to do?

What are they good at?

What do they dream about?

You get the idea. Create robust profiles for your characters – particularly your main character – flaws and all. And yes, your character needs flaws!

Don't think of the profile as something your character would show to the world. Think of it as a sketch or snapshot of who they really are.

As you're brainstorming, pay attention to your emotions. A sure sign that you're on the right track is when the character grabs hold of your heart.

It could be that you see part of yourself in them. Or maybe the character is struggling with a situation you've faced yourself.

The stronger your own emotional connection with the character, the better. And once you feel it, DIG. You're getting to the good stuff.

Can You Relate?

The second way is to START with emotion. Create a character who feels the way you do or did. Is there a deep emotion, a part of yourself or a memory from your younger days, that still speaks to you?

An emotional connection can be something painful like fear, insecurity, guilt, grief, feeling on the outside of things, feeling less than, feeling oppression, or being in need.

Or it can be something more positive like love or passion or loyalty or gratitude. It can be anything, as long as it's authentic to you. When it's authentic, your readers will relate.

That emotion is your way in. And once you're in, EXPLORE.

But be careful. Don't get too literal with it. Maybe as a kid or teen, you felt on the outside because your family didn't look like everyone else's. But maybe your character's reasons for feeling on the outside are totally different. That's where your imagination comes in. What you need to hold onto is the feeling, not the circumstances.

You'll know when you've found the right connection when you can't stop thinking about it. The idea of this character takes over your imagination. That's when you begin asking the important question — WHY?

Why does the character feel the way they do? How did they end up where they are? Brainstorm the answers. Lots of them. Don't worry about clichés at this point. As you clear your first less-than-brilliant thoughts from your mind, the really good stuff will come. That's when the magic happens.

After you feel good about your character's WHY, go back to their name, demographic info, personality traits and all the rest. Revise. Play around. Be creative, but make sure it all makes sense. Keep it cohesive.

Can I Get a Weakness?

Remember when we said readers want to relate to your character? They do. It doesn't matter if your character has a unique life situation, magical powers, or lives in a little-known place or point in time, readers want to feel what the character feels.

No, wait. They don't just want it, they INSIST.

The key to engaging your reader is to give your character an authentic and compelling voice. We'll talk a lot more about voice in Session 4. But for now, know that voice — the overall way your character tells the story, not just the way they speak — is the #1 way readers connect and relate to your characters and story.

The other is to make your characters 3-D. Give them strengths and weaknesses. Think: real traits that could belong to someone they might know — or better yet, someone they want to know.

Your character can literally have any strength or weakness you can dream up as long as it makes sense somehow. Your 17-year-old's skin can have purple polka dots if their parents both had the same recessive gene. Your mouse main character can read and write if they live in a 3rd grade classroom.

Don't forget that no one's perfect. Characters with flaws are a kabillion times more relatable than perfect ones. Maybe your character is impulsive or anxious or prone to stretching the truth. They might avoid conflict. They might make bad decisions. They might not know when to be serious.

Just make sure their weaknesses come from somewhere, like something that happened in their past or a way of coping with the present. The reader needs to get where the character is coming from. The all-important WHY. A character who lies all the time might come off as unlikeable unless the reader knows why they do it.

16

Like Blooms in Springtime

Finally, your main character needs room to grow. We'll focus more on growth in Session 6. For now, leave your character's emotional end point open when you're creating. You'll fill the ending in later. Trust that your character will not exit the final page exactly the same as they were at the beginning.

Growth can be "up front and in your face" as in YA coming-of-age stories. Or more subtle for younger readers. Who wouldn't cheer for the shy little bunny when they finish the first day of school? Or the anxious tween who finally sticks it to the green slime monster? Regardless of what change looks like, when a character grows internally, that transformation makes the story matter.

Dying for more practice on creating compelling characters? Head over to Session 6. When you're ready, we'll see you back at Session 3.

Tips and Tricks

- Create the character(s) that only YOU can create.

- Give your character a name that reflects something about them or gives the first impression you want to make.

- Play around with your character profile. It's okay to start out with blanks and fill them in later. The sketch often will change as you're writing.

- Interview your characters. Pretend you're their therapist(s).

- Do create character profiles for your other characters, especially your antagonist (more on this in Session 7), but don't feel the need to give them as much attention as your main character. It's not their book!

- Give every character a fun and interesting strength, a significant weakness, and a personal problem — big or small — even the secondary characters. It's the fastest and easiest way to give them depth and engage your reader.

- Limit your cast. Make sure every character serves a unique purpose in the story.

> The idea that not all stories are ours to tell, and not all characters are ours to write, is relatively new and definitely overdue. Before you embark on your writing journey, ask yourself, is this character's story mine to tell? Do my experiences and background equip me to tell the most authentic version of this story? Do I bring the nuances, the layers to make the character come alive? If the answer is no, or even "maybe," share your idea with an author who has lived those nuances. As kidlit writers, we have a responsibility to our writing community as well as our readers to ensure all feel secure and included.

Writing Exercise #1

Write a series of paragraphs where you put a character (Cinderella, The Big Bad Wolf, your own favorite or made-up character) in different situations. For example:

- They forgot to buy a gift for their best friend/beloved family member's birthday.
- They arrive at their secret place only to find their worst enemy/someone they are afraid of is already there.

- They meet a potential new friend who reacts rudely.
- They return home to find it mysteriously empty.

In each example, try to show either their personality, their passion, their strengths, or their weaknesses. Bonus points if you can show them all.

Writing Exercise #2

Brainstorm 10 reasons a particular character might be intensely afraid of:
- heights
- macaroni and cheese
- butterflies.

Writing Exercise #3

Fill in the blanks: A _____ named _____ is especially good at _____, horrible at ____, and doesn't want anyone to find out that they are secretly _____. Then write as many reasons WHY as you can think of. Then write 3 more!

Writing Exercise #4

Find an article or headline about a topic that interests you. Rewrite the content — a paragraph will do – in a way that adds heart. Hint: create a main character.

Writing Exercise #5

Two pups are lost.

Outline character profiles for one or both dogs, knowing that they want to find their way home. Try both approaches to creating stories with heart. Start with your imagination, then dig deep for your emotional connection to that character. Done? Great. Now start again – this time with an emotional connection to the story, setting or characters. Then layer on your characters' demographics and strengths and weaknesses. Which method works best for you?

Extra Credit #1

Answer the following questions in your notebook:
- Who are your favorite characters?
- In single sentences, 1 sentence per character, explain what makes them great/memorable.

Extra Credit #2

With a kidlit book you are currently reading or have already read, note the first 10 things the main character says or does. How do those first 10 things create an effective impression of the character? Make observations in your notebook.

Call to Action

Make reading new-to-market kid books part of your routine. Journal about the type of characters whose stories you'd like to tell. Don't settle on just one. Keep brainstorming. Have fun. Let your imagination go wild!

- Session 3 -
Are We There Yet?

> "Every story would be another story, and unrecognizable if it took up its characters and plot and happened somewhere else."
>
> — *Eudora Welty*

World-building

Which leads us directly to the topic of world building. And we don't just mean the rules of a world in a fantasy setting, although we certainly do mean that, too. We mean the whole freaking thing: 1) the place where your story takes place — the desert, Boston Common, Mars; 2) the time in which it takes place — today, tomorrow, the Dark Ages; 3) the nonphysical environment — the customs and values of the day; and yes, 4) the rules of the world in which the story is set — Harriet Tubman Middle school, Hogwarts, a leafless forest.

When you write a story, you get to plunge your characters — and your readers — into whatever world you choose. That can be a real place in the past, present, or future. It can be a made-up setting — ordinary or fantastical. Or a combination of the two. There's only one constant and it's a bomb — authenticity. Your world must be authentic. It has to feel real, whether it is or isn't. You want your readers to be immersed. You want them to suspend disbelief.

If your characters are animals, consider their circumstances. Are they pets? Captive? Do they make their home in someone's garage? Do they live in the wild?

If your characters are aliens, protozoa, or two brothers who share one brain. Same question: what are their circumstances?

The details can be as out there as you want. You're the creator. But no matter where and when your story takes place — even if it's your own hometown in the present day — be authentic. Do your research.

Even if you personally know this place, let's be honest – you are not your main character. They will experience the place differently.

Learn all you can about the environment. Read books and blogs. Watch videos. Go on a field trip. Do virtual searches. Interview people.

Of course, if you're writing Speculative Fiction and Fantasy (SFF), including Science Fiction, you get to create your own maps — not to mention the culture, political systems, and rules of society. Go ahead, nerd out!

In picture books, world building often happens in the illustrations. But that doesn't mean picture book authors are off the hook. To the contrary. You still need to convey your vision of the story's world through dialogue, action, and thought. If you can't "see" the story on the page, neither will the reader.

This Must Be the Place

An easy place to start building your world is in the physical. Where does your story take place? Which location? What environment? You get to choose.

Be thoughtful. In other words, pick a place for a reason. You may not hit the right location on your first try. No biggie. Try again.

In Cheryl's picture book, *Dario and the Whale,* the beach on Cape Cod sets the scene for Brazilian-born Dario to struggle making new friends. The fact that Dario's mom is a seasonal worker — a true, nonphysical attribute of that real place — adds depth to Dario's loneliness. When story and place are inextricably linked, you've hit your mark.

Time Flies

Time is one of the handiest tools in your toolbox. Time is everywhere. Seriously. There's clock time — a ticking clock creates suspense and feelings. Calendar time — the day, month, year. Calendar time can pin your story to a foundation. Seasonal time — seasons of the year create layers of association like spring with youth, winter with sadness and suffering. And historical time — the past does the heavy lifting by creating instant expectations of mores and customs. Think: 1820s, 1960s, or 1980s vs. today.

> Time is a great anchor for plot. A YA mystery might begin with senior year and be solved by prom or graduation. An MG crush at summer camp. A picture book where a character goes on an annual visit to see their cousins or grandparents.

U Can't Touch This

Think about the rules of behavior or codes of the society where your characters live — Think: customs and traditions. How do they speak? How do they dress? What technology do they use? How do they get around?

Even if your story is set in the present day, your answers may depend on which part of the world or country it is. Consider regional variations, differences among urban, rural, and suburban areas. Mountains or coastline.

Remember to think about social customs like those based on background, ethnicity, or religion, too.

And within those customs and traditions, where does your main character fit in? Consider their education, social standing, economic class, religious and personal beliefs, their neighbors, and wider community. It makes a huge difference whether they're on the inside or the outside, right?

Rules of the Road

No matter what world you write about — that universe must be governed by a reasonable set of rules. Even in fantasy, where magic dominates, rules matter. In *Harry Potter*, wizards and muggles co-exist. That's a rule. It's made up. Fake. Sorry.

To make the rule believable, Rowling had to create derivative rules like muggle-repelling and memory charms to explain those obvious times when muggles and wizards could clash. Without these rules, the UK of *Harry Potter*'s world wouldn't make sense.

And once you've set the rules of your world, please remember it is 1,000% critical that your characters obey those rules. If only vampires can teleport through doors, make sure your werewolf rings the doorbell.

Pardon a nerdy sci fi moment here, but who can forget "warp drive"? A make-believe fusion of gas and matter that results in space travel at a speed faster than light. True? No. Believable? Yes. Because Rodenberry had the genius to ground the fictitious chemical reaction in real science.

Tips and Tricks

- Rather than listing the characteristics of the setting, try summing up the details in one or two metaphorical lines. Examples: The forest was so empty, even the echoes seemed to have echoes. The forest was so quiet, the mockingbird had no one to mimic.

- Choose your setting for a reason — even if it's fictional. Write a story that could only happen in "that place."

- If you choose to set your story in a time other than the present, do it for a very good reason.

- Time — Fast vs slow. Fast forward through events that happen slowly in real life. For example: an ordinary bus ride to school or a routine night of homework. Slow your scene for things that happen fast in real life, especially if you want to spotlight a meaningful moment — a glance, a first kiss, a goodbye.

Writing Exercise #1

Describe the place in your fave kidlit story. No characters. No action. Start with a broad description. Give yourself a time limit (10 minutes) and don't stop writing until the time is up. Don't edit yourself. Just get the words down. Reread your paragraph and circle the words or phrases that resonate with you. These details are often the signposts for how best to convey your world to your reader.

Writing Exercise #2

Rewrite the paragraph in Writing Exercise #1 — shifting your focus to 1) the time factors, 2) the nonphysical factors, and 3) world-rules. Choose words that convey their emotional effect on the story. Example — Jill skipped up the hill and snatched the pail before Jack had bothered to tie his laces. Circle words and phrases that stand out.

Writing Exercise #3

Take your notebook to a corner of your home, yard, or another familiar area. Sit quietly for a minute. Write a paragraph describing the setting. Then, write another paragraph describing the setting from the perspective of an ant. Notice the differences in your paragraphs.

Writing Exercise #4

Choose a location that you know zero about — a mine on the moon, the inside of an atom, an oyster farm. Write a description of each place off the top of your head. Then spend some time researching the location and rewrite the description.

Writing Exercise #5

Write a whole paragraph about an ordinary bus ride. Then write that same bus ride as a single sentence. Write a kiss in a single sentence. Then write that same kiss as a whole paragraph.

Extra Credit #1

Amazon provides free access to the first few pages of most kidlit books. Search for books in your genre or with worlds that interest you. Tab to "Look Inside." Note how the authors introduce their world. Is it by place, time, customs, or rules? Or do they use other clever methods?

Extra Credit #2

Check out the reviews that books in your genre get on sites like Goodreads or Amazon. Notice any similarities in unfavorable reviews. Spoiler alert: The single easiest reason to dislike a book is because the world doesn't make sense.

Call to Action

It's time to start building your own world as a writer. If you haven't already, go to your library or search online for authors who are publishing in your category and genre. Browse their websites and social media. Read their blogs, sign up for their newsletters. Find out what people in your field care about. If you've already started the process, expand. Add ten more fellow writers to your list.

- Session 4 -
It's Good to Hear Your Voice

Voice

Voice is one of the most important parts of writing. Not only do readers connect with a character and story through voice, but voice is what distinguishes one book from another.

More than any other tool, voice conveys the style and tone of the whole story. Voice is what makes a book unique.

You may have heard that voice is instinctive or intuitive. True! Voice does come from within - but it's not necessarily a case of "you have it or you don't."

We're here to tell you that voice can be understood (Writing Exercise #1). And most importantly, voice can be found (Writing Exercise #2).

It needs to be found!

Voice is at the top of the wishlist for kidlit agents, editors, and publishers.

A huge part of finding your voice is deciding who will narrate your story. Whose perspective will you explore? From whose POV will you tell the story?

Just to get nerdy again, POV and perspective are often used interchangeably, but they're not exactly the same. POV refers to whether your narrator is giving a first-hand account of the story or is talking in the 2nd or 3rd person. POV also encompasses the perspective of that narrator, but it doesn't work the other way around.

Fenway and Hattie *is written from a dog's POV.* Fenway and Hattie *is written from a dog's perspective.*

Both are correct.

The students offered their POVs about Fenway and Hattie. *The students offered their perspectives on* Fenway and Hattie.

The first sentence is WRONG. The second is correct. Confusing, right?

Rule of thumb — If you can substitute "opinion," you mean perspective. Not POV.

Me? You? Them? POV

When you write in the 1st person POV (I, me, my), the narrative voice belongs to the main character ONLY — Think: every single observation they make, every perspective they share, and every internal thought comes from the main character. Writing your story in 1st person gives you the advantage of getting inside your character's head, immersing your reader in their perspective.

1st person is less popular in picture books than it is in MG or YA, although that trend is changing. Like older kids and teens, little ones are responding more and more to the instant and deep connection of being in sync with the 1st person main character.

2nd person (you, your, yours) is rarely used in MG or YA, but handy in PBs-especially those that "break the fourth wall." Today's metafiction is fun, edgy, and popular, at least for now.

When the PB narrator says to the reader, "Find the puppy," "Don't let your dinosaur forget her lunch," or "Try not to laugh while reading this book," they're talking in a 2nd person voice that "breaks the fourth wall."

> In picture books, illustrations contribute to voice. So do rhyme, meter, alliteration, repetition, and plot twists.

In 3rd person (he, she, they), the voice belongs to a narrator who is typically not one of the characters in the book. You have 3 options when writing fiction in 3rd person — omniscient, limited distant, and limited close.

Omniscient means an all-knowing narrator is telling the story. OG fairy tales immediately come to mind – *Once upon a time, there were 3 little pigs*.

But today's authors also love to use 3rd person, omniscient. Cheryl's picture book, *Elephants Walk Together*, is an excellent example. The omniscient voice narrates the story of Precious and Baba when they are together, as well as when they are apart. It's not just Precious's story and it's not just Baba's story. It's both of their stories, and the omniscient narrator allows the reader to experience BOTH of their perspectives.

3rd person, omniscient lets you give the reader access to the thoughts and motivations of any character you choose, including those the main character might not know about or events that take place outside their knowledge.

Sounds great, right? Not exactly. Omniscient narration can struggle to offer that close connection we were talking about in Session 2. But definitely give it a try. It might be the best way to tell your story.

3rd person, limited means the narrator is telling the story from only the main character's perspective, while using "he, she, or they/3rd person" pronouns. Example: *The little mouse Bertie was finally out of the boy's pocket. But he was not free.*

You can use 3rd person, limited in 1 of 2 ways — at a distance or up close.

With 3rd person, distant, the narrator is telling the story from the main character's perspective (Think: their slant on the story), but the narrator is not directly inside their head. Example: *The baby dinosaur was nervous about going to school. "I have a tummy ache," she said.*

Authors use 3rd person, distant all the time, particularly when they want to include scenes where the main character isn't present. Fun fact: 3rd person, distant is the POV in the *Harry Potter* books.

> 3rd person, distant
> *As she turned away from yet another disapproving look from her guardian, Leopoldia wished for the millionth time that her parents had survived the crash.*

In 3rd person, close (aka close 3rd), the narrator is still telling the story from the main character's perspective and using 3rd person pronouns, but the narration is basically the main character's "stream of consciousness." Like the narrator can go right inside the character's head and share all of their thoughts, observations, and opinions. Example: *Bertie hated avoiding his sister's question, but he had no choice. Their very lives could depend on it!*

This option offers many of the same advantages as 1st person, and yet might be more accessible to young readers. Close 3rd is a favorite of PB and MG authors who use it to build interest and heighten suspense while keeping the reader connected to the main character.

> 3rd person, close
> *Leopoldia watched Mrs. Whottle's face begin its usual sink into disapproval. She fought back tears. Why couldn't her parents have survived the crash? Then she wouldn't even know this horrible woman, let alone live with her.*

Having said all of that, there's no "right" POV to use in writing for kidlit, right? Correct! Choose what feels best for you and your story.

Don't Tense Up

Another element of voice is tense. Most kidlit is told either in the present or simple past tense. If you're using the 1st person, either tense works well. Examples: *I race around the room* OR *I raced around the room.*

If you're writing in the 3rd person, you probably want to use past tense. Example: *Raydon raced around the room.*

Present tense with 3rd person is less common, and risks making your story read like a screenplay or stage directions. On the other hand, it might be the next big trend. (Here's a secret: one of us loves 3rd person present.) Example: *Raydon races around the room.*

Picture books lend themselves easily to the past or present.

Two Sides to Every Story

Let's say that the most organic way to tell your story is through multiple POVs, like an essential back-and-forth POV between characters. If you plan to make multiple POVs part of your voice, each character's narration must be distinct to the reader (either 1st person or 3rd person).

Although we're into "breaking rules for a reason," we recommend keeping 1st person or 3rd person consistent throughout, meaning Ty and Meleena alternately describe what happened THAT NIGHT both in 1st person or 3rd person. Not Meleena in 3rd person, Ty in 1st.

We don't recommend breaking the head-jumping rule either. That is, don't head jump from the head of one character to the thoughts and opinions of another in the same scene, let alone the same paragraph. It's too confusing. Save those jumps for different chapters. And once again, make sure each character's POV and perspective read as unique.

Multiple POVs in picture books are less common. Not only do picture books lack chapters, but young readers love to identify with the main character. That's not to say that dual POVs in PBs are off limits. Only you can decide. Think: spreads (2 open pages) that go back and forth between 2 characters in 2 settings, for example.

Trust No One

If you think about it, every narrator is unreliable to some extent, right? No character, no matter how realistically drawn, is 100% objective all the time.

A narrator's unreliability can be part of the voice that makes your story appealing. Young readers love to feel "smarter" than the narrator. A perfect example is a picture book where the text says, "Tarvin saw signs that the puppy was warming up to him," while the illustration shows the dog chewing his slipper.

MG readers love when the main character realizes they've misunderstood a situation and the reader saw it coming. Young adults too love the tension of not knowing whether to trust the narrator. And that tension keeps them hooked.

All that being said, writing an unreliable narrator is tough. You have to pay close attention to the details to ensure that while the narrator may be lost or confused, the reader isn't. Or if the main character is intentionally misleading, that the reader is buying it.

> Unreliable narrators are... well, unreliable. If you decide your narrator is not always going to tell the truth or know the truth, do it for a good reason. Make sure the degree of unreliability you choose feels organic to the character and is the best way to tell your story.

Set the Tone

Tone is key to voice. The tone of your story comes from your choice of words. It puts your reader in a certain mood. It tells the reader a lot.

One tone might read light and fun or quirky, while another can sound dramatic, epic, or fantastical. Tone can be dramatic. It can be lyrical, rhythmic, poetic.

You can even vary your tone within the story, particularly in picture books. Think: using short, punchy lines to mimic quick actions. *He turned. He twisted. He had to get loose!* Choose longer, wordier sentences to reflect slower, quieter moments. *All afternoon, the spider was too focused on her web to notice the ants marching through the grass, the ladybug flitting from clover to clover, or the bees buzzing in the lilacs.*

Overall, consider the overall experience you want the reader to have and use a tone to match.

Variations on a Theme

Regardless of what you might remember from growing up, kidlit doesn't start out with a "message." Across categories and genres, books with heavy or stated messages are a huge NO.

But zero message can mean zero meaning, as in no layers (not good). Confused? Don't be. All we're saying is that while heavy messages are out, themes are in. In a big way.

Your job is to know your themes, the ideas that underpin your story and add authenticity to your voice. You can either weave them in as you're writing or you can think about them afterwards and add them in during revision. Either way, themes need to feel organic.

To identify your theme(s), ask yourself, "What is my story about?" or "What is the overall take-away from the story?"

Answer: friendship? bullying? unconditional love? Is it, "the grass is always greener?" or "there's no place like home"? For your story to resonate with readers, it needs to have at least one theme. But keep in mind that themes are best when they emerge subtly, like a lovely taste that lingers in your mouth, NOT a hammer that smacks you over the head.

Read our cover designer Wallace West's outstanding picture book, *Mighty Red Riding Hood*, for a great example of a theme that emerges naturally. We won't tell you what it is, though. Just read the book. We promise you'll get it.

Raw Voice

And lastly — if someone picked up your writing, could they tell it was yours? Does it sound like your voice? Is your writing dense? Spare? Are your sentences short or long? Do you use scads of dialogue? Are you drawn to a particular POV? The past tense? The present? A specific genre? Is your voice inviting, welcoming? Sharp and direct?

Exploring your raw voice is part of the natural process of discovering who you are as a writer and what you care about. Check out Writing Exercise #3 to get in touch with your raw voice.

Tips and Tricks

- Notice the POV in books you read.

- Try both 1st or 3rd person POV before you decide which feels best to you. Don't feel locked into either.

- When using 3rd distant, think of the narrator's voice as an unseen character.

- If your story involves time-hopping or flashbacks, you might want to use present tense in those moments so it's clear to the reader when the story is moving back in time.

- Play fair with the reader. Indiscriminate mixing of a fantasy voice here, a detective voice there, will confuse them.

- Find your narrator's or main character's voice during the pre-writing stage. Ideally, you shouldn't begin your first draft until you have that voice down. However, if your instinct tells you to jump right in, go ahead. But understand you'll be rewriting your first few chapters a few times to give your main character's voice a chance to set.

Writing Exercise #1

Take each of the following mini character sketches and ask the character the suggested questions one at a time. Write long-winded responses AS the character responds (in either 1st person, 3rd, or with each). Let the character ramble in their own unique voice. Don't edit. Don't force it. Let the character's voice emerge. Notice that the voice can reflect a tone that's dramatic, funny, mysterious, or magical, etc.

Character A: Shanford A. Tuttle
A 12-year-old boy. Lives in a small town in the midwestern USA with his parents & pet canary named Lollipop whom he's obsessed with. Shanford is extremely introverted, clever, and has a big imagination. He's impulsive and deathly afraid of lightning storms.

Character B: Lola Ledbetter
A 16-year-old girl. Lives in a big city in the southern US with her grandmother & 8-year-old twin brothers named Remo and Nico. She is outgoing and loves to dance. She's determined, doesn't take rules too seriously, and desperately wants to be famous.

Character C: Cheese Doodle
A mouse who lives under the porch of either Shanford's or Lola's home (your choice). Cheesy took refuge there after being chased by a broom. Now he longs to be reunited with the rest of the Doodle Mouse family.

Suggested questions to ask each character:
1. What do you dream about?
2. What did you do yesterday, how did that turn out, and how did it make you feel?
3. If you could magically change one thing about your life right now, what would it be, why, and what difference would that make?

Writing Exercise #2

Take this story idea — Eulalia kills her first dragon and assumes the throne of Springfield - and write a paragraph.
When you're finished, rewrite the paragraph 3 out of these ways:
- From the former throne-holder's POV.
- In a different tone.

- In a different tense.
- With the location changed from Springfield to the International Space Station.
- With Eulalia as an animal and the dragon now a human.
- Knowing that Springfield is on the verge of sinking.
- Or that the kingdom next door — Poshfield — is raking in major coinage with their newest money-making scheme: spinning straw into crypto.

Writing Exercise #3

Pretend you're writing a letter to a friend. Tell them a story that you don't have to think about too hard — what your niece or kid or grandchild just did, a familiar children's book, the plot of your favorite movie, something that really happened to you — in your own words. Don't edit yourself. Let the story flow naturally as if you are talking.

If you have trouble letting go of your internal critic, try some of these strategies:
- Write in the dark or with your eyes closed.
- Use meditation, breathwork, or relaxation techniques to clear your mind before you start.
- Write outdoors near grass, pine needles, or wild herbs – engage your senses.
- Dress all in white.
- Play instrumental music.
- Set a timer and don't stop writing until it goes off.

The point is to free yourself. Let go. Only then can you hear what's in your heart. Write that.

Writing Exercise #4

Rewrite each of these sentences in a spooky tone. Then rewrite them in a silly, dramatic, or somber tone.

The quick brown fox jumps over the lazy dog.
My very excellent mother just served us nachos.

Writing Exercise #5

Zoe has just turned 12. Her story/theme is loneliness. Write a quick summary of her story WITHOUT using the words: lonely, sad, unhappy, cry, alone, sole, isolated, or empty, or any derivatives. Fun, right? How does her story end?

Extra Credit #1

Pick 5 kidlit stories in your genre published within the last 3 years. Answer these questions about each one:
- Which POV does the author use?
- Who is telling the story?
- What qualities make the voice unique? How would you describe the voice if you were writing a review?
- Pay extra attention to the first chapter (or first 10 pages). What does the voice reveal about the character?
- Jot down ten sentences or phrases that establish the tone. How does the tone fit with the genre?

Extra Credit #2

Pick your two favorite kidlit stories of all time and note the elements of voice that make you love them. Note the differences between each author's style. Then write a summary of one story in the voice of the other author.

Call to Action

Continue to get to know yourself as a writer. Keep a journal with observations as they relate to voice. Do you connect most strongly to certain types of POV, tense, tone as a reader? As a writer? As you complete the writing exercises, what are you learning about yourself? How unique is your writing voice compared to what you are reading? Are you starting to feel drawn to a certain style of writing?

- Session 5 -

"Let's Chat."

Dialogue

Of all the tools in your toolbox, dialogue is the one you grab first. Not only do all those quotations and white spaces draw the reader's eye to the page, but dialogue is an organic way to introduce personality and voice.

Rina: "I don't care."

Shannon: "Remind me, why I should care?"

Haylan: "Does this really matter?"

Galla: "I'm outta here."

Toni: "Caring's not a concept that intrigues me enough to embrace it."

Knox: "Why on earth should I bother with that?"

There's no better way to move the plot forward than through dialogue. "You wait here. I'll check the barn." Even backstory can be woven into dialogue. But slowly. Do it in bits to avoid the dreaded info dump, where too much information renders the conversation inauthentic.

> Info dump: "Hey, did you see Jean, my uncle who crashed his car last year and broke his leg in 3 places?"
> Better: "Hey, have you seen Uncle Jean? He's still limping."

Dialogue Do's and Don'ts

Do begin a new paragraph every time there is a new speaker, even if they only utter one word.

Do use a comma to introduce dialogue or when a dialogue tag follows a quote. Put periods, question marks, exclamation points inside quotation marks. Here's a quick guide:

> Shue said, "I demand we go to the beach!"
> "Let's go to the beach," said Shue.
> "Let's go to the beach."
> "Should we go to the beach?" asked Shue.
> "I demand we go to the beach!" Shue said.

Do watch your dialogue tags (also called narrative tags). Think: standard words that indicate who's speaking. Words like "said" and "asked" are so ingrained in today's lexicon that readers zip right past them and zoom in on what's being said.

Do use "said" and "asked" most of the time. The last thing you want is for the reader to stumble over a narrative tag.

Here are some great big DON'Ts:

> "Hi, Vimmy," she smiled. (You can't smile, hello.)
> "Hiya, Shue," he winked. (Nobody winks anymore. Plus, you can't wink, Hiya.)
> "Guess again!" he laughed/wept. (Laughing and weeping do not describe the act of speaking.)

Do make it easy for the reader to follow. Kidlit readers want to know who is speaking — fast. When the first clause of the dialogue is complete, insert a narrative tag with a period, as in, "Listen up," said Vimmy. "We're going to the beach." Don't stick the tag at the end of a long, windy sentence: "Hello, Vimmy, let's go to the beach for some fried clams and French fries and ice cream, and then we can eat them," said Shue.

Do mix action tags in with your dialogue. Nothing bores a reader more than the same sentence structure over and over (noun, verb object). Stretches of unbroken dialogue can be even worse (dialogue, tag, period).

Check out this sequence of dialogue. Meh, right?

> "Where are you going?" Rhetta asked.
> "To the festival," Vemy said.
> "Why? We went there yesterday," Rhetta said.
> "Why do you care?" Vemy asked.

What if we drop in some action tags?

> Rhetta crossed her arms. "Where are you going?"
> "To the festival," Vemy said.
> "Why?" Rhetta shook her head. "We went there yesterday."
> "Holy crap, Rhetta, why do you care?"

Better.

Do use internal dialogue — Think: a character's thoughts, as opposed to their actions or spoken words — to keep your reader engaged. Readers are dying to know your character's ideas and opinions, the slant through which they view the world. They crave it. A story without little or no internal thought is a missed opportunity to grab your readers' attention.

> Jumping juniper, today's the day, Wylie thought. He couldn't wait to get to school.
>
> Marshall shimmied farther under his blankets. Nuts! Today's the first day of school!

Note that in close 3rd or 1st person, the reader is in the narrator's head, so internal tags are not necessary.

Thoughts are never put in quotes. Ever. Quotes are exclusively used to signal the spoken word. Some writers italicize their characters' thoughts. Others don't. Just be consistent.

Let's Talk Picture Books

Some picture book texts are 100% dialogue. Some don't use any at all, for example counting books and other concept PBs. And then there are wordless PBs that rely on illustrations to create dialogue in the readers' mind. Still other PB writers incorporate dialogue as refrains, repetition, and rhyme.

Tips and Tricks

- Give each of your characters a unique speaking voice.

- Read your dialogue out loud to make sure it sounds natural.

- It's not necessary to use dialogue tags ("he says/said," "she asks/asked") each and every time, but make sure it's easy for the reader to follow conversations and know who is speaking.

- Purists insist writers use only "said" and "asked". Others (like us) don't mind a change every now and then, like "called," "cried," "shouted," and "explained." Careful not to overdo or confuse.

- Avoid using adverbs in your dialogue tags unless 1,000% necessary. *"Come here!" he shouted frantically.* NO! The adverb is redundant. *Yvonne thrust out her arms. "Come here!"* YES!

- Dialogue is not a phonographic reproduction of the way people actually talk. While you ARE trying to capture the cadence of speech, there's no point in including non-helpful idioms in conversations. *"Like, you know, uhh, like aaah maybe that wouldn't be such an umm sterling idea."* No.

- Pay attention to the expressions that people use and the music of everyday conversation. But avoid trendy slang which will date your story.

- Limit how much info you put in your dialogue. It shouldn't be obvious to the reader that they're being fed important facts.

- Think about the difference between characters who say, "I dunno." vs. "I haven't the foggiest notion." Keep your character's voices authentic.

Writing Exercise #1

Convert the following into dialogue without narrative (passages of text). Use dialogue only.

Jack was nimble. Jack was quick. Jack prepared to jump over the candlestick. Juanita swiped it at the last second.

Writing Exercise #2

Take the trying-on-the-glass-slipper scene from Cinderella. Pick one POV character — the Stepmother, the stepsisters Drizella or Anastasia, the Prince, or Cinderella and write a chunk of dialogue. Afterward, ask yourself the following questions: Does the dialogue feel authentic? Have I struck the right mood? Have I conveyed what I want to say in the best possible way? Is there anything I can do to tighten the dialogue? Do I believe what the characters are saying?

Writing Exercise #3

Rewrite this snippet of dialogue, varying the sentence structure and inserting dialogue and action tags to make it more interesting and more visual.

> "We can't just break into Dr. Madbunny's lab, Gio."
> "We're not going to break in. We're going to sneak in."
> "I hate to bring you back to reality, but we're going to get caught."
> "Oh, Leith, you're such a scaredy cat. I'm not sure how we're even friends."
> "I ask myself the same thing."
> "Which changes nothing. So let's get on with it."

Writing Exercise #4

Take the dialogue you've written in any of the previous writing exercises and reverse the speakers. Have the asker be the listener. The first speaker becomes the second. Play around. Try it on a second piece of dialogue. And a third. See what you can tighten or eliminate.

Writing Exercise #5

Rewrite the following passage, incorporating dialogue to reveal Jodpu's personality and state of mind:

> *Jodpu cast his line into the sea again. It had been eighty-four days now without so much as a sting. (Bonus points if you got this nod to Hemingway's* The Old Man and the Sea.*)*

Extra Credit #1

Take your two fave kidlit characters and experiment writing dialogue between them. What would Dorothy say to Cinderella if she could? Change the POV and see what happens. Take notes. Home in on the voice that seems more natural to you.

Extra Credit #2

How do other kidlit authors write dialogue? Make a point to browse your local bookstore, online vendor, or library, and page through kidlit books randomly. Check when the first sentence of dialogue appears. The first page? Opening line? How much internal dialogue happens in the first scene? The first chapter? Take notes!

Call to Action

What better way to nail dialogue than to listen to what real kids say and how they say it? So go ahead. Next time you're in a coffee shop or fast-food hang out, on a bus or subway, at a playground or ball game, eavesdrop. Absorb the vibe. Take notes on actual conversations. Listen to words, tone, and note physical gestures. Of course, be mindful of the privacy of others!

- Session 6 -
So what?

Story Problem/Character Arcs/Stakes

Every story needs 3 things – a problem to hook the reader, arcs for the main character, and stakes. Full stop.

Getting to the Root of the Problem

The story problem can be a big problem, like a city threatened by an evil genius or a priceless treasure that suddenly goes missing. Small problems work too, like a teen who wants a date to homecoming or a squirrel who needs to prep for winter. No matter the size, the story problem is the overall ACTION conflict of the story, the main character's action quest.

To identify your story problem, answer this question: What does my main character want?

The main character wants to save the city, find the treasure, get a date, or fill their storeroom with nuts. The outcome doesn't matter as much as the problem. For example, the squirrel can FAIL to fill their storeroom, provided they find another way to survive the winter.

The story problem should be resolved in the climax - the final and main confrontation between the main character and the antagonist. (More on antagonists in Session 7. More on climaxes in Session 10.)

> In MG and YA, every story has a story problem, meaning a problem that your main character actively tries to solve.
> To find your story problem, ask yourself:
> What does my main character want?
> What do they need?
> What do they lack?

Make your story problem something your reader cares about. Think: a problem that's personal and relatable, NOT a quest to find a case of missing bearer bonds they heard about on the news.

The story problem has to have consequences or stakes. When the stakes matter to the main character, they will matter to the reader. Stakes are so important we're going to explore them separately in this session.

And lastly, you need to know WHY your main character cares about the story problem. In other words, your character needs motivation and that motivation needs to make sense.

Sometimes, you start out with the character's motivation, so you know it from the start. Go, you!

More likely, you'll discover the WHY as you're writing your first draft, or during those long interviews with your characters, or yes, possibly in a clue that's been cluttering up that messy closet in your character's room.

Don't worry. The WHY will come to you, and you'll have your story.

The story problem can change over the course of the plot, provided each successive problem logically and causally leads to a bigger conflict.

Tension must escalate. Conflict needs to grow. The problem solved in the climax should be the most contentious, emotional, highest stakes problem in the story.

The secret to success looks like this: Hook the reader with your story problem. Make them care. Get them invested. And create the tension that keeps them reading.

Some story problems are so intriguing they've become iconic.

- *Harry Potter*: Can Harry find the Chamber of Secrets in time to save Ginny and defeat Voldemort?
- *A Wrinkle in Time*: Can Meg find her scientist father before he's lost in time forever?
- *The Giver*: Can Jonas escape the deadly restrictions of his utopian community in time to save Gabe?

Learning Curve

Your characters will charm their way into readers' hearts when you give them 2 arcs.

The first is their action arc. As the name implies, the action arc is when they start out at Point X and in the course of solving the story problem physically/action-wise end up at Point Y.

You've probably guessed that the story problem drives the action arc. In other words, the main character goes from Point X to Point Y in their quest to solve the story problem.

The second is their emotional arc or their internal journey. The main character begins as flawed and then changes in a positive way (Think: growth) by the end of the climax.

Can a character change for the worse? Possibly, but if your main character spends the story becoming evil or narcissistic, why would the reader keep reading?

The emotional arc is driven by an unspoken story question — the question that stems from the character's emotional wants or needs. The unspoken story question creeps into the reader's mind early on, creates tension, and pulls them through the story.

Sienna is a talented drummer (strength) who vomits every time she's the center of attention (weakness). Will Sienna overcome her condition, or will she let it ruin her life? (unspoken story question).

Here's a geek-out question — Can you name a kidlit character who doesn't have an emotional arc? Answer: Nancy Drew! Good old Nancy stays emotionally and physically stuck at the age of 16 (or 18 — she ages 2 years in the later series) for 175 volumes. Suffice to say, Nancy would not get published today.

Not only should the unspoken story question be age-appropriate, but readers must relate. In the first *Harry Potter* book, the unspoken story question might be: Will Harry ever belong? Or will Harry ever find a real family? In a romance, the unspoken story question is usually: Will the heroine ever find happiness? Not — will she end up with Felicia? That's the story problem. See the difference?

The unspoken story question also needs to feel authentic to the character.

Jenia suffers from anorexia, she's mild mannered and shy. A wall flower. Subconsciously, she controls her eating in an effort to disappear from an abusive situation at home. Jenia's unspoken story questions might be: Will she ever be safe? Will she find peace?

Zill suffers from anorexia, too. But unlike Jenia, she's outgoing and loud. Her parents' expectations are off the charts. It's Harvard or nothing. Zill captains the debate team. Her goal is perfection. Her unspoken story question might be: Will Zill ever find her real self?

Gosh, we hope so! Not only do both characters feel authentic, but the unspoken story questions are unique to each and equally compelling.

Let's look at those iconic story problems and explore the related, but unspoken story questions.

- Story problem: Can Harry find the Chamber of Secrets in time to save Ginny and defeat Voldemort?
  Unspoken story question: Did the Sorting Hat put Harry in the wrong house?
- Story problem: Can Meg find her scientist father before he's lost in time?
  Unspoken story question: Will insecure Meg shed her negative self-image in time to save her family?
- Story problem: Can Jonas escape the deadly restrictions of his utopian community in time to save Gabe?
  Unspoken story question: Will Jonas have the strength to change his world?

What's at Stake?

Stakes are the answer to the question, So what? Consequences make the reader care about the story problem and the unspoken story question. If the main character doesn't solve the problem or if the unspoken question doesn't get resolved, disaster strikes. Oh, and by the way, if disaster doesn't strike — your reader will stop caring.

Pro tip: To make your stories shine, overlap your action arc and the emotional arc and ratchet up the stakes.

In *The Lightning Thief*, if Percy doesn't find Zeus' lightning bolt, a war will break out between the gods that will end the world (action stakes) and he'll never be accepted by his real father, Poseidon (emotional stakes).

In *The Wizard of Oz*, if Dorothy can't go home to Kansas, she'll be stuck in Oz forever (action stakes) and she'll never see her family again (emotional stakes).

In *Cinderella*, if Cinderella doesn't get home by midnight, she'll be outed as an imposter and punished by her stepmother (action stakes) and she'll never have a happily-ever-after with the prince (emotional stakes).

> The stakes have to be big enough to carry the story. But high stakes don't have to mean life and death. It's the intensity of the main character's desire that drives the stakes, not the violence or magnificence of the desire itself.

Having told you that your story will sizzle if your main character has overlapping arcs with high stakes, let's take a look at *The Hunger Games*, Book 1. If Katniss doesn't win the game, she will be killed, her family and planet will remain under tyrannical rule. Super! Story problem, action arc, and action stakes — all 3 nailed. FAB!

But what about Katniss' emotional arc and the unspoken story question? Does she shed her stubbornness in Book 1? Her bitterness? Her lack of faith in anyone but herself? Not really. Katniss's emotional arc doesn't end until the series ends — with her expressing genuine love for Peeta. Despite the enormous success of *The Hunger Games*, we still recommend you include a highly charged emotional arc for your main

51

character in each book of your series. All of the story elements — story problem, arcs (including the unspoken story question), and stakes–should be present at the series level *and* in each individual story.

Now let's put it all together using the example of drum-playing Sienna:

After stage-frightened Sienna solves the mystery of her missing drum kit (initial story problem) in time for regionals where she's playing in front of her Hall of Fame, absentee father for the first time (stakes), she discovers her music is stronger than her fears (unspoken story question/emotional arc) and rocks out a drum solo that annihilates the competition (action arc/final story problem).

What About Picture Books?

Do picture books have story problems? Action and emotional arcs? Stakes? Yes and no. Mostly yes.

The easiest way to capture a reader's attention is to create a loveable main character, assign that character a want or desire that matters (story problem), and let them loose on the page.

A young koala dreams of becoming a juggler and overcoming his fear of failure (story problem/unspoken story question). After conquering obstacle after obstacle, he reaches his goal (arcs, stakes) but in a surprising way.

> Lucky PB writers have more options than their MG and YA counterparts. If they don't want to rely on a story problem, they can use tools like structure, humor, verse, alliteration, rhyme, repetition, and or twists to create the pulse that drives the story forward.

Tips and Tricks

- Even in PBs, your main character needs to be the one to solve the story problem. They can have help, but they must be the hero of their own story. (We honestly can't say this enough.)

- A good way to flesh out the character's emotional arc is through the subplot(s).

- Begin your story when something changes or is about to change. This change sets up the story problem.

- Your character's action and emotional arcs should end in a place 180 degrees opposite from where they started. Pro tip: begin with your character's endpoints. Then flip them around to find your starting points.

- Set up the stakes early in the story. Page 1 is not too early.

- Raise the stakes at least once over the course of the story.

- The stakes of your story problem or your unspoken story question can be clear, such as the good guys win, or the bad guys win. But a conflict where your reader doesn't know which outcome to root for, as in the case with a love triangle or a moral dilemma, also makes for great storytelling.

- Raise the stakes by raising the consequences of NOT reaching the goal, or by making the likelihood of reaching the goal harder, or both.

Writing Exercise #1

Severance Mayhew is currently holed up below deck on a sailing ship to the New World. Identify 5 different possible story problems. Hint: What does Severance want? Focus on action. Pick your favorite and write a paragraph, fleshing out the problem.

Writing Exercise #2

Toby can't figure out why his friends keep disappearing. Maybe the new principal has something to do with it. After all, she does seem to be double jointed. And those buggy eyes...

Assume Toby wants to find his friends. That's the story problem. In order to find his friends, Toby has to do x. Identify 3 different action arcs for Toby, note them by starting point and ending.

Example: In his home laboratory, Toby analyzes the DNA on his missing best friend's sweater. In a heroic last stab, Toby plunges his mother's knitting needle through Mrs. Bugella's exoskeleton.

Pick your favorite and explore.

Writing Exercise #3

Greer can't face another day at Dunesville High. Her girlfriend dumped her. She was caught tagging a car. And her parents are still living in the 2010s. All Greer wants is to get out of Dunesville. When her SAT scores mistakenly come back as 800s, she...

Name your story problem (remember Greer wants out of Dunesville) and set the action arc. Now, identify 3 unspoken story questions and brainstorm Greer's emotional arc.

Pick your favorite and write.

Writing Exercise #4

With any of your choices above, put together your main character's profile. Add in some worldbuilding — time, customs, rules. Choose strengths and weaknesses that enable your character to answer the story problem and unspoken story question.

But don't make it too easy. If Greer can fly, withstand bullets, and read minds, her trip out of Dunesville is assured. What fun is that?

Seriously. In the context of the story problem and unspoken story question, what attributes does your main character need to succeed?

Writing Exercise #5

Add major stakes to the following. Hint: What does the main character want? What happens if they don't get it?

- Lin is a foot soldier in Emperor Xtren's army. He vows revenge on the Emperor and all that the robot stands for.
- Baby Skunk is embarrassed by her stripe. She admires Squirrel's beautiful gray coat.
- Two grasshoppers set out on a journey to find their families.
- Whatever that thing is in the lake, Jenna can feel its pain.
- As if looking out for his little brother isn't enough, Geoff has to clean the house and pay the bills. Why can't Mom be like everyone else?

Then, whatever stakes you've created, double them. Up the ante.

Extra Credit #1

Pick any kidlit book. Identify the story problem, the unspoken story question, and the stakes of each. Notice if the story problem and/or the stakes change over the course of the story. And if they do, how?

Extra Credit #2

Make the story in Extra Credit #1 your own. Keep the world and the character the same. Change what the character wants. That is, create a new story problem. What is the character's new action arc? Emotional arc? Tie the emotional arc to a new unspoken story question. Make it make sense. Pile on the stakes. Jot it all down.

Call to Action

Story ideas are lurking everywhere! With your new writer's eye, scope out your environment and journal one new story problem a day for 10 days — no days off! Stick to your genre or let your imagination run loose. Spend the next 10 days brainstorming 10 main characters who can solve the respective problem. Over the next 10 days, develop unspoken story questions for each of those characters and their story problems.

If a particular story idea intrigues you, ditch the rest of the assignment and focus on that.

- Session 7-
Being Bad

Antagonists

Who doesn't love a really great bad guy?

For good reason. Without bad guys, there are no stories. And by bad guys, we don't mean just villains. We also mean events, governments, and situations that throw speed bumps into the main character's plans. Layer in the main character's inner conflicts and feelings and you've got kidlit gold.

In short, antagonists are anyone or anything that creates obstacles to the main character's goal (story problem). Focus on creating great antagonists and you'll be swimming in stakes, tension, and conflict.

Exterior antagonists — true baddies — are fantastic to write. In addition to villains, oppressive leaders and unfair political systems make the top 10 of exterior antagonists.

Interior antagonists - Think: the character's own faults, failings, prejudices, insecurities — are equally VERY COMPELLING. Contemporary YA and MG readers love stories that focus on internal failings rather than a single baddie. Fear, false beliefs, guilt, rage, and mental health issues set the main character against the most powerful foe imaginable, themselves.

What really elevates kidlit is a healthy dose of both — exterior and interior antagonists.

Aaron's sister needs medicine, and he's determined to get it (story problem). If all Aaron has to do is ride his bike to CVS and pick up the prescription, there is no antagonist and so, no story. But throw a mountain into his path (external antagonist), and the fact that the medicine is a white lacy flower that blooms once a year (external) — on a cliff guarded by a witch (external), and meanwhile, Aaron is paralyzed by heights (internal). Well, now we're talking story.

Another way to create delicious tension is by shifting power from one antagonist to another or between the main character and the antagonist. In *Harry Potter*, Professor Quirrell and Severus Snape make powerful antagonists in their own right, but the big shiver happens every time Voldemort appears in a scene.

Power takes many forms – physical strength, charm, knowledge, moral power, wealth, ownership, rank. It can also take the form of weakness — need, illness, passivity — that is, manipulative tools that can prevent the main character from achieving their desire.

Without doubt, strong antagonists make for a strong main character, and a strong main character makes a good story. So set up your roadblocks and make them bad. The more you develop your obstacles, including your main character's inner faults, the more your story will become real. And the more the reader will root for your hero.

> If the feedback on your story is that it lacks stakes, reexamine your antagonists. Are they believable? Are they bad enough? Can they stop the main character from reaching their goal? When the antagonist is highly motivated to act or highly motivated to avoid the outcome desired by the main character, you've got a winner.

Bad to the Bone

Getting up close and personal with a villain is good. *Scratch that* — getting personal is great.

A villain with a deeply personal quest to make sure the main character fails is the best of the best. Remember, there are two sides to every story. Your antagonist has one, and it's legit.

Be thoughtful about assigning your villain their own action arcs and emotional arcs. Give them feelings and needs, and at least one likable trait. Everyone likes puppies and kitties, right? Everyone has a mother, a sister, a best friend who helped them on their journey. Even totalitarian governments might spare the life of a rebel or two.

Bad guys with no feelings, no needs, and no desires fall into the realm of comic book characters. Which is okay... if you're writing a comic book.

What drives your antagonist? What's their situation in life? Backstory? How do they view the main character at the outset of the story? How about over the course of the story as your main character makes bad decisions, messes up, or otherwise fails? Are the two acting against each other? Matching strength with weakness and weakness with strength? Or are they similar?

Harry Potter bases whole plots on Harry and Voldemort's sameness. Sameness creates competition in the reader's mind, which in turn ratchets up the tension and conflict. If Harry and Voldemort are both super strong and way smart, who will win?

Brrr

Can weather be your antagonist? Yes, but...

Weather is the bad guy in so many stories, it risks becoming predictable. How many teens have gotten snowed in at the ski cabin? How many roads have conveniently been washed out right when the hero is about to reach the final destination?

Now, we're not dismissing the real, horrific damage that weather causes. We simply want to challenge you to use that blizzard or flood in an original way. Maybe it was created by an alien or an evil scientist. Make your antagonists clever, interesting, and fresh.

Pop quiz: Deka is trying to locate the priceless gem that — according to legend — sank to the bottom of the treacherous Lake Lulu. Finding the gem is Deka's only hope

---

of paying off her parents' debts and keeping them out of prison. Which one of these is the antagonist?

A. A drifter who also wants the gem.
B. Deka's best friend who thinks Deka takes too many risks.
C. Deka's broken arm.
D. Deka's inability to swim.

Read on for the answer!

Like Onions

Remember that readers love main characters with layers. Don't forget to use your character's internal weaknesses as antagonists.

Know the origin of the failings and flaws that are holding your main character back. Make sure the physical manifestations are relatable and authentic. Know where the internal roadblocks come from. Make sure they make sense.

Place your main character's weakness front and center in the story. An inner flaw that is not big enough or developed enough to stop your main character from achieving their goal is not going to cut it.

Weaknesses are good, mind you (see Session 2), but your reader wants to see them early and often, and understand how they're blocking your character's path.

For Victoria's character Fenway, his love for his girl Hattie is both his greatest strength and his greatest weakness. He'll battle evils like squirrels and delivery trucks to keep her safe, but his fear of losing her love leads him to do things that actually push her away.

Friendly Fire

Friendly characters can also be antagonists. Think about it: A well-meaning parent can be working against the character. "It's not safe for you to go to the sleepover." "You're too young to go to the dance."

A best friend can be an antagonist, too. "I can't let you do it. You promised you wouldn't." Their teams can go head-to-head in the playoffs. They could be trying out for the same role in the play. One can have a crush on the other's ex. You get the idea.

A teacher or coach or mentor can be an antagonist. They might create difficult tests for the character to pass before they can move on to the goal — even if the tests are for the character's own good. The Wizard of Oz tells Dorothy he won't help her go home until she brings back the broomstick of the Wicked Witch of the West.

> Any character that makes it harder for the main character to achieve their goal is an antagonist.

Child's Play

By now, you know every story needs obstacles. But the younger the audience, the less overt the antagonist. For obvious reasons, Voldemort is not going to show up in a counting book about unicorns.

PBs that don't incorporate antagonists rely on more age-appropriate methods of creating tension: repetition, rhyme, meter, refrains, twists, alliteration, and especially surprise. These tools pull the reader through the story and keep them coming back.

A great example is *Goodnight Moon*. While there is no internal or external overt antagonist, repetition and rhyme keep sleepy heads listening to the very last page. Other PBs with non-traditional story arcs keep the readers' interest with structure (Think: one thing builds on another, a circular structure that comes back to the beginning, or the course of a single day) or concepts like counting, ABCs, or colors.

Just for the record, if you read closely enough, you'll find that most PBs actually do incorporate at least one age-appropriate obstacle. A dog meets a friend who refuses to play and turns out to be the dog's reflection in a puddle. One little monkey hogs the bed from the others. A girl's shyness gets in her way on the first day of kindergarten.

And... you've probably figured out that the pop quiz answer is all of the above. They each create obstacles to Deka's quest, so they are all antagonists.

Tips and Tricks

- Create character profiles for your antagonists. Know their background, origins, strengths, weaknesses, and goals (wants or lacks).

- Make sure your story's internal and external antagonists are properly developed and not 2-dimensional cardboard speed bumps.

- It's nice - particularly in a story for young readers - if you decide to have the antagonist(s) pop back in at the end having grown or changed off-screen, especially when they give credit to the main character for making them better individuals.

- DO remember your story can have MANY antagonists, not just one.

- Make a list of all the possible antagonists for your main character. When you get to the middle of your story, refer to this list (and add to it) to create scenes/conflicts for your main character.

- Plot-driven stories and genre fiction — stories where action dominates — often involve your antagonist driving the story problem. The main character has to stop the antagonist's evil plan or else.

- Character-driven stories — stories where the character's emotional journey plays the major role — tend to involve antagonists trying to stop the main character from accomplishing the goal.

- The higher the stakes — either the main character wins or the antagonist wins–the better, the story.

Writing Exercise #1

Insert 3 age-appropriate antagonists as obstacles into the following PB scenario:

The sun rose over the little farm. Conroy, the cow, and Henri, the horse, spend the day eating grass. At dusk, the stars appear and the animals bed down for the night.

Hint: Start with a story problem. Once you do, the obstacles will appear in your head as if by magic.

Writing Exercise #2

Pick an object or person in your life and turn them into a villain. Write the first 9 villainous traits that pop into your head plus one good quality. No editing. Now brainstorm their arch enemy - your main character. Are the two characters equals? Is one more powerful than the other?

Writing Exercise #3

Start developing a list of internal antagonists/character flaws. Focus on the ones that resonate with you. Over your writing career, this list will become your best friend. Start creating characters that go with the flaws. As your character list grows, so will your list of story problems/ideas.

Here's what we mean:

Flaw	Name	Story Problem
Shy	Benjy Sixpence	Benjy refuses to wear shoes.
Guilt	Tonya Williams	Tonya wants the lead in the school play.
Anxiety	Max Hampton, III	Max hacks into the CIA's anti-USA file and discovers his mother is on it.
Addicted to video games	Jessie Jennings	Jessie is a D1 caliber athlete.

Writing Exercise #4

Turn the following seemingly good deeds into obstacles.

"Let me clean up your room," said Mom.
"Need help with that science project?" Dad asked.
"When's the bake fair?" Nana said. "I'll make your favorite chocolate twists."

Writing Exercise #5

Toddler Becca is on a rampage. She WILL keep that stuffed hedgehog, the one Dad let her hold to keep her happy in the shopping cart.

Think of a fresh, fun ending. Becca is our hero, no matter how much she acts up. And as the hero, even in a PB, she has to solve the story problem herself. Hint: Give Becca some redeeming traits — she's kind, she shares, whatever.

Extra Credit #1

List your top 10 favorite villains, from literature and the movies. What do you love to hate about them?

Extra Credit #2

Find 5 villains in kidlit published within the last 3 years – how do they compare to your classic favorites?

Call to Action

In your notebook, start brainstorming the antagonist(s) of the century. Who/what are they? Are they bad? Could they be badder? Does your antagonist have at least one character trait that makes them likable or at least relatable?

- Session 8 -
Once Upon a Time

Plot vs. Story

Ready to get nerdy again? We're going to talk you through plot and story. We like to think of plot as the who, what, when, where, how and why of the story. The logical sequence of cause-and-effect events that transport your reader from point X to point Y. If you were to make a list of every scene in your book, and jot down a few lines summarizing what happens in each scene, then string those summaries together, to us, that's plot.

We think of story as a broader concept. Yes, it incorporates the who, what, where, how, and why. But it also includes your characters and their POVs, perspective, and strengths and weaknesses. Their world and arcs, their voices. Don't forget the story problem and the unspoken story question.

In other words, story is everything.

An easy way to wrap your head around plot and story is to consider how a news story differs from a fictionalized account of that same story. One gives you the information you need to understand the issue. The other does all of that, plus engages and entertains you.

When you start querying — Think: sending your manuscript out to agents or editors — you might be asked to submit a 1-page synopsis of your plot. In that case the agent or editor will be expecting not just the sequence of events, but the totality of the book — voice, backstory, setting, tone, character(s) and their arcs, stakes, and theme — as well as the plot. In other words, the story. Now you know!

Here's how plot and story fit together:

What does your main character want? (story problem). Why do they want it (motivation)? What steps does your character take to achieve their goal (plot)? What will happen if they fail (stakes)? What are they like at the end? (emotional arc). What has changed emotionally? (unspoken story question).

Not to downplay the importance of plot. Plot matters. Not only do the characters' action steps (plot) create the roadmap to your story, they also anchor the arcs and stakes. Without a series of logical steps linked by cause and effect (plot), there would be no story. All we're saying is that when asked to summarize your PLOT, don't leave out the good stuff. Tell your STORY.

No surprise, story is the secret sauce in picture books. Young audiences have short attention spans. They want to be engaged. They want to be filled with wonder. A recitation of events is not going to cut it. To add richness to the story, picture books feature tried and true kid pleasers: alliteration, rhyme, rhythm, repetition, twists, and/or humor. In Cheryl's *Dario and the Whale*, she weaves the story problem (will Dario make friends with the whale?) and unspoken story question (will he ever fit in?) into the plot and wraps them all in a dose of lyrical repetition.

PLOT: Because Alice is curious about the White Rabbit, she follows him through the rabbit hole. Because Alice then finds herself facing a hallway of locked doors, she searches for a key. Because Alice finds that the key opens the tiny door, she opens it. Because Alice longs to visit the beautiful garden she sees through the tiny door, she eats the mushrooms and shrinks...

STORY: Alice, a bored girl picnicking with her sister, notices a White Rabbit dashing by. Curious about the White Rabbit, Alice follows him down the rabbit hole. The simple warren she expected is actually a hallway of locked doors. Anxious to explore, Alice finds a key but it's too small for her big fingers. It isn't until a disagreeable caterpillar induces Alice to eat mushrooms, that she shrinks and unlocks a tiny door to a beautiful garden. From there, she encounters the Mad Hatter and his never-ending tea party along with the unreasonable Queen of Hearts...

Insert Clever Subtitle Here

Most novels, even in kidlit, have at least one main plot and one subplot and usually more. Subplots – also known as secondary plot threads or storylines — are workhorses. They make the story richer, more complex, and more satisfying. Not only that, they also develop the main character and secondary characters, complicate the main plot, raise the stakes of the main plot, and help provide context. Phew! (Are you exhausted yet?)

Pro tip: One key difference between a chapter book and a middle grade novel is the absence of subplot(s).

Case in point — Victoria threaded not one, but two action plots into each of the *Fenway and Hattie* middle grade books. In addition, each plot also has its own subplot. In Book 1, Fenway's quest to regain Hattie's friendship is his main plot while his struggle with the Wicked Floor is the related subplot. Hattie tries to get Fenway to behave (her main plot) while she attempts to make a new friend (related subplot).

In contrast, each title in Victoria's much younger chapter book series, *Make Way for Fenway!*, features only one straightforward plot. For example, *Fenway and the Bone Thieves* is simply about Fenway's quest to get his bone and keep it all to himself.

Tips and Tricks

- Pitches and synopses are meant to be read as stories, not plot summaries.

- Conflict and tension in your plot should follow an upward trend, gaining in intensity until the climax. If the sequence of events does not continue to worsen, you might lose your reader.

- If while writing your manuscript, you hit a wall. Chances are the problem is NOT your plot. It's your story.

- In that case, go back and reevaluate your characters for strengths and weaknesses, including (especially) your antagonist. Then turn to your story problem (what does your main character want?). Is it big enough? Does it need to evolve? If your main character solves the story problem on page 30, your book is finished. Make sure your characters have arcs that track with the unspoken story question. And stakes. By all means, pile on your stakes.

- Think about plots and subplots as pieces of a jigsaw puzzle. They must intersect.

- Your main character should actively drive the plot in at least 70% of the scenes.

- Each of your plotlines should "appear on the page" in proportion to their weight in the story. The main plot carries the most heft. Subplot(s) less.

Writing Exercise #1

Rewrite your fave kidlit story as you would expect to see in a newspaper account or a photograph accompanying the article. Focus only on plot.

Writing Exercise #2

Rewrite the plot above as a one paragraph story. Get creative. Go rogue! What differences do you see?

Writing Exercise #3

12-year-old Cici Gurigliaro is trying out for the last spot on the state soccer team. Now write a one paragraph story where your antagonist is another 12-year-old girl who wants the same spot.

Writing Exercise #4

Sasha, the Siamese cat, has a knack for solving mysteries. The trick is to get everyone else to do the work. Her current case involves the appearance of a deep hole between the house Sasha lives in and the next-door neighbor's.

The story problem is that Sasha must solve the mystery. Your cast includes but is not limited to: the Great Dane next door; a local contractor; a neighborhood trouble-maker (also a cat-hater); and a family of woodchucks.

Brainstorm two different subplots. Focus on how they tie into the action plot — who did it? — and move the story forward.

Writing Exercise #5

Familiarize yourself with any version of *Jack and the Beanstalk.* Then using no more than one sentence each, describe each of the following beats:
- The main character
- Story problem - initial and final
- Unspoken story question
- Antagonist
- Stakes
- Plot (Pro tip: semicolons are the way to go)
- Subplot - If none, can you think of one?

Now combine your sentences (excluding the subplot) into a readable, entertaining, one paragraph summary of your story.

Extra Credit #1

The ability to condense your entire story into one riveting paragraph is an art. What do you include? What do you leave out? One answer is to research what your favorite authors/publishers say about their book in the marketing blurb on the back or how the book is described on the publisher's website. Every publisher lists their catalog of books on their website along with gorgeous pics of book covers and professionally written blurbs meant to attract the target audience.

Extra Credit #2

Pretend you are the head of a major publishing imprint that focuses on your category. You and your staff are committed to getting quality books into the hands of as many children as possible. This year, the budget only allows for 3 publications. Brainstorm which 3 books — content wise — you would choose to provide maximum sales and still stay true to your mission. Impersonal decisions like this are what drive book acquisitions. Not the quality of your writing.

Call to Action

Just about anything can be turned into a story. Like your day, for example. Spend a few minutes thinking about EVERYTHING you did today. Then list your activities in detail. If the list reaches the floor, start curating. This assignment doesn't depend on accuracy. Once your list is done, look for sequences of causes and effects. If you don't see any links — because of x, main character does y — make them up. Add a main character from your genre and genre-appropriate dialogue. Insert a problem or an antagonist. Add fun details.

– Session 9 –

Behind The Scenes

Scenes

Now that you get plot and story, let's dive into scenes. Scenes are the building blocks of story, how it unfolds on the page. When each scene is stacked and stuffed with goodies like dialogue, stakes, and conflict, the reader will be hooked all the way to the end.

How do we define a scene? A scene is a concrete event or time period with a clear beginning, middle, and end. In the beginning of the scene, the main character enters with a specific goal. In the middle, action happens. At the end, something changes.

That last point is super important. Every scene ends with a change. If nothing changes as a result of what happens in the scene — or if the change is a repeat of a previous scene — that scene doesn't belong in the story. Each scene needs to pull its weight. It needs to earn its way into the story.

Plus, there has to be a logical link between scenes, like the sequence of cause and effect in plot. That doesn't mean scenes have to follow in chronological order. But it does mean scenes must causally link together - because of what happened in Scene A, the characters do x in Scene B. Or Scene J.

All of your scenes need to be strong. There's no room in the story for weak links!

> Q: How many scenes do you need in a whole novel?
>
> A: As many — or as few — as you need to tell the story. There's no ideal number of scenes in YA or MG the way there is for word count.

Think of each scene in a book like a mini-story with a setting — place, time, world — and a main character, typically the main POV character (but not always). IN EVERY SCENE, the main character must have a goal. Something they want a lot. As in stakes. An antagonist or obstacle must stand in the way. Action happens – usually with surprises or twists – until finally, something changes.

> Pop quiz: Is this a scene?
>
> A. *Bale breezed into school, a smile on his face. The swim team was going to Regionals! He opened his locker, stuffed his backpack in, and went to class.*
>
> B. *Bale went to his locker. He saw the principal walk by. He ducked his head to avoid her. He heard her footsteps heading in the other direction.*
>
> C. *Bale was at his locker when Mrs. Perez walked up. By the look on her face, he knew she knew. He had to throw her off track. He couldn't jeopardize their chance to go to Regionals.*
>
> *"What's up, Mrs. P?"*
>
> *"The swim team's GPAs jumped 5 points," she said. "Do you know anything about that?"*
>
> *"Of course not." He zipped his backpack. "Wait - why are you asking me?"*
>
> *The principal folded her arms. "We have ways of tracing digital activity, Bale. It's only a matter of time before we ID the culprit." With that, she headed down the hall. Bale gulped. He had to warn the guys.*
>
> Answers:
>
> A. NO. Reason: Setting? Yes. Main character? Yes. Goal? No. Not a scene. Full stop.
> B. NO. Reason: Setting? Yes. Main character? Yes. Goal? Yes. Stakes? Unclear. Antagonist/Obstacle? Yes. Action? Yes. Change? No. Not a scene. Full stop.

C. YES. Reason: Setting? Yes. Main character? Yes. Goal? Yes. Stakes? Yes. Antagonist/Obstacle? Yes. Action? Yes. Change? YES. It's a scene.

Here's WHY scenes need to check all these boxes - the reader needs to know when and where they are in the story. Along with which character to follow and what to root for. Otherwise, they will be lost, confused, or even worse, bored.

Beyond that, the reader wants tension. Will the character achieve the goal? Or will the antagonist derail them? As the scene concludes, the change that happens moves the story forward and keeps the reader turning the pages.

Are Scenes Seen in Picture Books?

Yes! Because picture books are typically 32 pages, the scenes need to fit logically within that format. Sometimes one scene appears on each double spread - the open book, double page, lying across your lap. Other times, you may see a scene continue over multiple spreads or vice versa (more than one scene in the same spread). 10-14 scenes per PB is common, though not a hard rule. If you need more scenes than that to tell your story, think about the short attention span of the audience. Then make your final decision.

You also need to remember that page turns usually coincide with the end of a scene, signaling the change that causes the little listener to want to see what happens next. Twists are surprises, like punchlines, that typically happen at the end of the story. Most often, the twist occupies a full page. Successful twists both delight the reader and elevate the story. If you are a text-only picture book writer, you have the tough job of conveying your vision of the entire story – every scene, every spread, every page turn, and every twist, while leaving room for the illustrator to express their vision in the art.

By Design

Remember, your reader wants to live vicariously through your main character. That means they need to be able to picture each scene in their mind. So give your scenes a cinematic quality — design them as if the events are happening in real time.

Include well-chosen descriptive details that help the reader imagine the scene. Then add well-written dialogue, with its accompanying white space, to move the reader through the scene. Don't forget well-placed narration to keep the reader in the story. Vary these 3 elements — description, dialogue (including internal), and narration — as you see fit, keeping in mind that changing things up keeps the reader alert.

Know the infamous rule, "show, don't tell?" It means to write by design or "in-scene" whenever possible, especially during important moments. In other words, use language like a video camera. "Show" the reader what is happening. Don't tell us. At the risk of repeating ourselves, write as though you're making a movie or painting a picture with words.

TELLING:

I walk into the room. I smell the bone on the counter. I remember that I love bones. I want that bone. But the counter is high. I can't reach that high. I want to figure out a way to reach it. Or convince someone to give it to me. I have to have that bone!

SHOWING:

I burst into the room, my tongue dripping. Sniff, sniff... *My nose detects a tasty bone on the counter. Wowee! My teeth want to chomp into it! Oh, but there's a problem - the counter is way up high. Oh, how can I reach it? I need that bone! Hey, maybe I can convince someone to give it to me?*

TELLING:

The whole ride home from school, Mom talked non-stop about the PTA fundraiser. I stared out the window until she asked point blank if I was listening. I didn't want to admit I had tuned her out, so I did what I usually did. I lied.

SHOWING:

The whole ride home from school, Mom said things like, "I have so much to do" and "It's going to be the best auction ever" and "blah, blah, blah." I listened for as long as I could stand it, until counting the passing houses got more interesting. "Sami?

Earth to Sami! I asked you a question." I knew from her tone I'd been busted. "I heard every word you said, Mom," I lied, again.

Pop quiz: Show or tell?

A. *Donata saw the tracks. They made her sick.*

B. *Donata got onto all fours to examine the prints in the fresh snow. The width of the pad and the point on each toe told her the cat weighed more than she did.*

C. *Taric did not want to jump into the quarry. It was an accident waiting to happen.*

D. *"Oh, come on." Taric ran both hands through his hair. "Seriously? You expect me to jump into that?"*

E. *Bunny didn't know where she was. She was scared.*

F. *Bunny shivered under the dark leaves. "Mama?" she called.*

Answers: A. Tell, B. Show, C. Tell, D. Show, E. Tell, F. Show.

Having said all that, a quick line of explanation at the right time might be a better way to communicate with the reader, rather than showing, so that the reader doesn't have to take their mind off the story.

> *A chill ran through my body when Mr. Gonzales walked in. He'd given me a F in US History last year. What could he possibly want from me now?*

A long "showing" scene of what happened in History class last year would be a flashback and would take the reader out of the moment. In this case, telling the reader what they need to know, that Mr. Gonzales had given the character an F in History last year and nothing more, gives the relevant context while keeping them in the scene.

Behind-the-Scenes: Shh!

Let's talk quiet scenes. Slowing the pace of your story at times gives your characters and your readers a moment to regroup. Think: scenes with lots of interior dialogue and/or low-level emotion and/or little physical action. Not only do quiet scenes help characters (and readers) process what's happened so far, but a lull in the action is a fantastic opportunity to reveal more about your character and their inner world.

Pro tip: quiet scenes make a perfect set-up for your main character's critical AHA! moment at the start of Act 3 when they typically undergo a period of self-realization. (If you're intrigued like we are by beats and milestones and where they go in your story, jump ahead to Session 10 —The Anatomy of a Story. Go on. We'll wait.)

Say you're writing a YA urban thriller and your main character Jaron just shimmied out of a dangling elevator. In the next scene, a quiet, reflective Jaron might be shooting hoops while he thinks back on his narrow escape. Or, out in Space Garrison 141, Vivian, the out-spoken niece of the commander, might be watching her twin nephews while she runs through a list of clues and realizes her uncle is the killer. Clearly not every scene needs action that moves at 100 mph.

Now you may be wondering if quiet scenes need goals, obstacles, and a change at the end. They DO. No matter how lovely your description or authentic your interior dialogue, if the goal, obstacle, and change are nowhere to be found, you don't have a scene — quiet or otherwise.

The obstacles can be as quiet as the goal. Let's say Jaron's goal is to catch his breath — after all, he almost died. Maybe self-doubt makes him miss shot after shot until he gives up. Or out in space, maybe one of the twins drags Vivian into the virtual playground, making it impossible for her to think.

Or maybe... MWWWWAAAAA. Jaron's stalker texts a live pic of Jaron's sister doing her homework. Or Vivian's uncle taps her on the shoulder.

Like every other scene, the change at the end of a quiet scene should propel Jaron or Vivian to take the next step in the plot.

Behind-the-Scenes: Hello, Goodbye

Opening scenes are the hardest to write. Expect to revise your opening many, many times. Typically, your story starts with your main character living their life, on the eve of some big change.

Your job is to introduce the reader to your character's "here and now" before the change. And show your main character doing something — emphasis on the words DOING SOMETHING — that spotlights their personality and reveals one of their strengths. Don't forget to hint at their major flaw and allude to the story problem or outright identify it, along with the stakes. All while hooking the reader and without dumping in a ton of backstory.

Oh, and by the way, your opening sentence needs to grab your reader. It needs to get their attention, connect, and make them want to keep reading. So no passive verbs — *Juniper was munching on a leaf when the wind blew.* No bland impressions — *Carla opened the car door.* No telling — *This story changed Tuna's life.* No boring exposition — *The ship docked at the marina before the passengers embarked.* Your opening sentence is your handshake with your reader. Don't make it a limp one.

Here are examples of opening lines that pop:

Juniper clutched the trembling leaf with all six feet, hoping to avoid the fate of her siblings.

Carla swung the car door open, thinking only of the hot vinyl seat, not the body on the floor.

Tuna trembled before the vision of herself in the cloud. What happened next would change her world.

The clipper ship slipped into the dock unnoticed by all, except one - the only one that mattered.

Closing scenes tell the reader what happens after the main character and antagonist have clashed in the climax and completed their action arcs and emotional journeys. Final scenes often mirror opening scenes in location, tone, or by theme, like the opposite bookend on a shelf. And of course, they will give the reader the happy — or at least hopeful — ending they've been waiting for.

Behind-the-Scenes: Backstory and Flashbacks

Accept the cold, hard truth — you want to write backstory and flashbacks more than your reader wants to read them. Sorry, not sorry.

When you absolutely have to write backstory, give only as much information as needed and in as engaging a way as possible. Make sure all of it is relevant. Bits of backstory dropped into the story's present-day dialogue or internal thought can round out your character and add depth, so long as what happened in the past doesn't slow the forward movement of your plot.

Flashbacks are tricky. Very few people can recall a scene from the past as if they are literally reliving it. Everyone changes and grows over time, so looking back on the past happens through the lens of perspective. Which means for a flashback to work, you might consider incorporating some telling.

Use the scene immediately before and after the flashback to decide whether you are going to tell the reader what happened entirely or write the flashback completely in-scene. Think: Show it in real historical time as if the reader was actually there.

Behind-the-Scenes: Prologues & Epilogues

Like backstory and flashbacks, prologues and epilogues can be sticky. Try your hardest NOT to use a prologue or an epilogue. Try to incorporate whatever happens before the story starts or after the story ends into the story itself. Most prologues make better Chapter 1s.

But if you decide you can't tell your story without them (or either of them), go for it. You do you.

Tips and Tricks

- Create a map of your scenes (Writing Exercise #1) to see your story at a glance.

- Think about blocking scenes as if you're a theater director. Set the stage, put all the characters in their places, know when each is coming in or going out, where and how the action will happen – you get the idea.

- How to write a scene in 2 steps:
  1) Set up the scene and show the reader what they need to know, including what the character wants and why.
  2) Put yourself into the main character's head and act it out.

- Resist the urge to "info dump" in a scene. Think of info dumps as piles of rocks weighing down your rowboat.

- Having said "show, don't tell," never underestimate the power of juicy bits of telling when they're short, interesting, and you handle them right.

- Use the final scene to tie up loose ends.

- If you know how your story ends, go back and rewrite your opening. Make it 180 degrees from the ending.

- Use backstory and flashbacks only when you've "earned them." Think: when you've created so much curiosity in the reader's mind that they're dying to know "what happened" in the past.

- When writing a flashback within another scene, either show the scene and tell the flashback or tell the scene and show the flashback.

Writing Exercise #1

To make a story map of your scenes, grab some note cards, yellow stickies, a picture book dummy, or a spreadsheet and summarize what happens in each scene or spread. Practice on your fave kidlit book. In as few words as possible, identify the setting of each scene (high school caf, under a mushroom), the main character, the main character's goal in that scene, the antagonist/obstacle to that goal, the stakes, what action happens, and the change.

When you make your own story map, understand you don't have to wait until each scene is perfect or your book is complete. A story map is a living document. Leave spaces. Change your mind. Use your map to cut redundant scenes or add characters (or erase them). No one is going to read it but you.

Writing Exercise #2

Turn the following "tells" into "shows."

- Davi felt sad.
- The horses were starving. They hadn't eaten in a week.
- The bus left without Lorcan. He was so mad he put his backpack on the ground.
- "Don't do that, Kipper," said Jada energetically. "Sit still."
- The little church was on the hill.

Writing Exercise #3

Posabel secretly "borrowed" her nana's magic pencil this morning. Last summer, Nana told her the pencil magically writes brilliant answers to any question. Today is the big science test. Her teacher, Mr. Toughgrader, gives the hardest tests ever. Whoever scores 90% or higher gets free tuition to the Elite Summer Science Camp. Attending that camp is Posabel's dream. But Posabel's family can't afford to send her. As Posabel walks into the classroom and opens her backpack, she can't find the magic pencil.

In single sentences, describe 3 opening scenes and 3 closing scenes.

Writing Exercise #4

Now rewrite (and embellish) the above prompt using only SHOWING but TELL the part about what happened last summer.

Rewrite (and embellish) the above using only TELLING, but SHOW the part where Posabel walks into class, thinking about the camp, thinking about Mr. Toughgrader, and then looking for the pencil.

Writing Exercise #5

Using the prompt in Writing Exercise #3, write 10 killer opening sentences.

Extra Credit #1

Go back to the titles you've already read. Reread them as a more experienced writer. Note how the authors handle scenes. Make a story map of the first 3 spreads (PBs) or first 25 pages (MG and YA). Pay attention to the opening scene. Does the author hit the checklist? Main character, trait, voice, world, story problem, stakes?

Extra Credit #2

If you're leaning toward a prologue or an epilogue, research other books that have them. Are they common in your genre? If your readers gobble up prologues like goldfish (the crackers, not the fish), read those published prologues carefully and compare them to their respective first chapters. Note the differences. Is the prologue in the past? Chapter 1 in the present? Is there an obvious connection between the prologue and Chapter 1?

Call to Action

Consider this assignment as a mini pat on the back for making it this far. Only one session left! Take some time for yourself. Grab a glass of something appropriate and kick back with a great book.

- Session 10 -
The Anatomy of a Story

Structure

Spoiler alert: We are SUPER NERDY about structure. We love teaching it, talking about it, and obviously, using it.

A strong structure grounds your characters and plotlines and builds and maintains tension. But most of all, it keeps your reader turning the pages.

We're obsessed with the 3-act structure of plot (and yes, we mean the sequence of action events in a story). Not only do we use the 3-act structure ourselves, but we recommend it to everyone — especially beginning writers.

We know there are tons of opinions on structure out there. But we happen to think our version is accessible and successful.

Still, learn all you can. Then, like every other aspect of writing, if your story needs to be told within another structure, go for it.

So now without further ado...

The 3-Act Structure of Plot

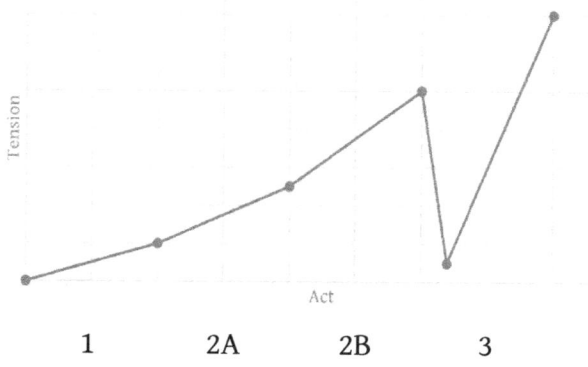

Every story can be divided into 3 acts. Act 1 is the first 25%, Act 2 is the next 50%, and Act 3 is the final 25%. To keep things even, we like to split Act 2 into 2A and 2B, with the end of 2A being the story's midpoint. Each of these 4 parts takes up the same amount of real estate in your book, but they each serve a very different purpose.

Role Playing

Here's the role of each act.

Act 1 is where the story starts. It represents "the before." Act 1 gets the reader hooked. The reader meets the main character as they are, in their normal life circumstances, engaged in their main passion, and showing their strength, or main personality trait.

The unspoken story question begins to form in the reader's mind. And then POW... something changes! An incident occurs that kicks off — or "incites" — the story, the story problem and its stakes.

The action of Act 1 escalates until the end of Act 1 when the main character faces a major turning point (Turning Point #1), literally a point from which there is no return to life as it was "before."

Act 2A is where the "real story" starts. Now the reader is invested. They want to see what the main character will do. The main character tries and fails to solve the story problem while the antagonist(s) is working against them.

By now, all the subplots are established (if not already established in Act 1). Act 2A ends with another turning point, (Turning Point #2) the midpoint, that raises the stakes.

In Act 2B, the plot thickens! Now the reader is flipping pages faster because the tension is higher. The stakes are much greater so it's more important than ever for the main character to solve the story problem. The antagonist(s) make life more and more difficult.

Tension spikes to another turning point (Turning Point #3) where the main character has their best shot yet of solving the story problem, but then the worst possible thing happens. The main character loses and the antagonist wins. Disaster! The reader is shocked, surprised, and dying to know how the main character will react.

Act 3 begins with the character's lowest point where they ask, "How did I get into this mess?" They are forced to face their own flaw(s) and failures. You might hear this moment referred to as the Day of Dark Soul or the scene where All is Lost.

But guess what? The story isn't over — the story problem hasn't been solved. So the main character has to regroup, and after a moment of self-realization (their big Aha!), they discover the only way out is up.

The character then takes the first step toward the climax (where they will solve the story problem). Facing multiple, tougher obstacles, overcoming them all, possibly with the help of friends, the character finally confronts the antagonist and solves the story problem and answers the unspoken story question (Turning Point #4).

All subplots wrap up and the story is over. The reader is totally satisfied. YAY! They recommend the book to all their friends. THE END.

Put Down the Markers

Sounds simple, right? In a way it is. Think of the 3-act structure as a road map or a frame for your story. How you use this scaffold is up to you. YOUR creativity dictates the fun and the richness and the complexity and the uniqueness of your story.

Let's take a deeper look at the milestone markers within each act.

Few stories begin with the main character's birth. Most of the time, the character has been living their life up to a certain point until a change occurs that sets the opening scene in Act 1. Okay, we're hooked. We're reading along when – BAM – that incident we mentioned above happens, the incident that incites the story.

Here's where the story problem starts. Mysterious letters come to Harry Potter's aunt and uncle's house. Miss Gulch seizes Dorothy's dog Toto and plans to have him destroyed. Fenway discovers that things are missing from his family's apartment. The inciting incident happens early in Act 1. The exact moment doesn't matter, as long as the event launches the main character on the road to solving the story problem.

How do you know if your event is the inciting incident or simply another scene in Act 1? Ask yourself, "Because of this incident, is the character's life-as-usual changed forever?" If yes, you've nailed your inciting incident. If no — life would continue as is — you need to find another inciting event to kick off your story. BUT FOR those letters arriving at the Dursleys, Harry would never know he was a wizard. He would never go to Hogwarts. That's why the letters are the inciting incident.

The first 3 turning points — end of Act 1, the midpoint, and the end of Act 2B — are points in the story from which there is no going back. Each of these points changes everything. Harry gets on the train to Hogwarts. Dorothy lands over the rainbow. Fenway realizes that Hattie is changing in a way that does not include him.

The last turning point (#4) is the climax in Act 3. The climax doesn't happen until the second to last scene or chapter in your book. It's the emotional high point of the story — the payoff for the reader. At the climax, the main character uses their strength(s) plus everything they've gained or learned over the course of the story (including help from friends) to overcome their main flaw and solve the story problem.

> Climax: All that has happened, all that the main character has gained or learned in the course of the story, empowers them to triumph (and BTW, you get to decide what triumph means) over the antagonist, solve the story problem, and answer the unspoken story question.

The climax doesn't have to be a violent showdown, but it does need to be hard for the character. Think: they have to face their greatest fear, they finally have to tell the truth, or they have to face up to a reality they've been avoiding for their entire life. Whatever the climax is, it has to matter. A lot.

After the climax, the main character and the antagonist are forever changed. Mostly for the better. Note: Stories can end with the main character's failure so long as they resolve the story problem.

The resolution (last scene) comes after the climax. The story is over. It's the grand finale where the reader gets to see how everything has changed for the better. The main character is living their "new normal." If you go with a happy ending, the future is bright. If your story is dark, your main character may have failed, but the story problem and unspoken story question are resolved. In addition, all the loose ends (subplots) are now tied up.

Milestones at a Glance

Act 1	Act 2A	Act 2B	Act 3
Opening scene Inciting Incident End of Act 1 - Turn 1	Main character tries and fails - all subplots present Midpoint - Turn 2	Antagonist winning End of Act 2B - Turn 3	Day of Dark Soul Journey to Climax Climax - Turn 4 Resolution (last scene)

Picture Books

You might be surprised to learn that the 3-act structure fits organically with traditional picture books. In the beginning (Act 1), we meet the main character, the world, and the story problem. In the middle, a series of obstacles stops the main character from achieving their goal (Act 2) until the end, when the main character confronts the antagonist (climax) and solves the problem, hopefully with a fun twist (Act 3).

Tips and Tricks

- Make a list of all the potential antagonists for your story and the obstacles they can cause. Use the list to brainstorm conflicts for your main character in Act 2.

- Don't forget to raise the stakes at the midpoint.

- If you already know your climax, you can actually plot backwards. For example, say that at the climax of your story, your main character will navigate a series of boobytraps and use her expert skill to disarm the bad guy's explosives. Knowing this ending lets you plan earlier scenes where your character studies the ins and outs of explosives, learns how to get around the various boobytraps (or gains allies who have those skills), and start the story with strengths that might include resourcefulness, cleverness, and a passion for electronics or machines.

- Note that high stakes don't have to involve the threat of World War III. It's the intensity of the character's goal that drives the impact of the negative consequences of not getting there. For example, if your main character needs to earn the top spot on the soccer team to have a chance at a scholarship or she can't go to college, the danger of getting caught cheating can be life-changing for her.

- The pace of your story can vary. Not every scene needs to be full of riveting action. Go back to Session 9 to see how to write quiet scenes. Giving the reader a chance to catch their breath, especially after intense or deeply emotional moments, makes sense. But make sure the quieter scenes are carrying their weight and moving the story along overall. If you aren't hitting your milestones at the right places in the story, your pacing will be off.

Writing Exercise #1

Lillicent is a young badger who lives in an underground burrow with her clan. Every evening, Lillicent and the other young badgers wake up and forage for food. But one night, everything changes.

Write 10 possible inciting incidents (the "everything" that changes) that could kick start a story.

Writing Exercise #2

12-year-old Darcet's mother - his only family - is rapidly declining from a mysterious illness. They have no insurance and no money for medical care. They live in a rural area where their only neighbor is an eccentric doctor. A storm threatens, the area is under a tornado watch and the power is out, phone lines are down. Darcet's mother tells him that the doctor is actually a werewolf. She is hallucinating. Or is she? If this is Act 1, come up with 10 choices that Darcet can make that could qualify as Turning Point #1.

Writing Exercise #3

Xiev wants to win tickets to the first-ever, one day Slimefest at The World of Slime. His idol, Adeno Jackson, the famously reclusive inventor, is going to be the grand marshal. Xiev wants to meet Mr. Jackson and show him his own invention — a contraption that could turn broccoli into chocolate bars, if only he could get it to work. It's missing one critical piece, and Xiev knows Mr. J. can figure it out. Xiev needs his invention to work because...

- Brainstorm 3 different ways to complete the last sentence (the stakes).
- Assume Xiev meets Mr. J. at Turning Point #2, the story's midpoint. Brainstorm 3 events that raise the stakes and qualify as a point of no turning back for Xiev.

Writing Exercise #4

Berta, an only child who's always longed for a pet, brings home a strange egg she found in a quarry. The egg hatches and a young lizard crawls out. Thrilled, Berta keeps him. At first, everything was great. But then the lizard keeps growing. And growing. Pretty soon, it's clear that Berta's pet lizard is actually a T. Rex! Her parents decide to donate him to the museum. But Berta can't bear to part with her T. Rex, who by the way, is enormous, so she sneaks him into her family's barn, telling her parents that he ran away. Little does Berta know that her parents are planning a surprise party for Aunt Myla in the same barn. Assume you've written to the end of Act 2. List 3 events that turn Berta's deceit into disaster, Turning Point 3.

Writing Exercise #5

In a final climax scene (Turning Point #4), 12-year-old Sani confronts the witch. Outline how Sani triumphs and the resolution to the story. To give you space to create, we've deliberately left out the story problem, other characters, Sani's strengths and weaknesses, and the unspoken story question.

Extra Credit #1

Take any novel and analyze its structure. What is the inciting incident? What is the turn at the end of Act 1? What happens at the midpoint (literally halfway into the page count)? How and when do the stakes get raised? What happens at the end of Act 2? What happens at the climax? (Hint: *Harry Potter and the Sorcerer's Stone* is a good book to use as an example.)

Extra Credit #2

Reread any 3 picture books, old or new, fiction or nonfiction. Find each story's climax, that scene where the action quickens, and the emotional quotient hits its peak. Note how the main character's actions answer the story problem. Compare the first scene to the last scene. What's the same? What's different?

Final Call to Action

Well, here we are. You did it. You finished the course. Kudos! Our goal was to give you the tools and insights to help you write the book that's in your heart AND the book that kids and teens want to read. We hope we've done that.

We've loved having you here over these past 10 sessions. We love cheering you on. We love sharing nerdy stuff, tips and tricks, and everything in between. And part of the reason why is that we know it works. We have books on our shelves right now that our former students have published. Won huge awards, even. Soon, one of those could be yours!

Writing for kids has its challenges, and one of the biggest is actually sitting down and putting in the effort.

Of course writing kidlit also has incredible moments of grace. To know your picture book is being read aloud to toddlers, to find your middle grade novel dog-eared in a library or discover your YA story has touched the heart of a teen – is profound. No other type of literature leaves a bigger impact on its audience or its authors.

And while writing is an activity that we do by ourselves, we want to leave you with the message that writers need to community. We ought to know!

So yes, please, join a critique group, subscribe to kidlit organizations, many of which are free, follow other writers on social media, support them and they will support you. Follow the industry news as it relates to sales, changes in the publishing, and other topics that interest you. Participate in kidlit conferences, workshops, and fellowships if you can. In essence, reach out and be present. Don't be afraid to say yes!

And in a final FINAL call to action: Carve out that elusive moment of alone time or meet up with the friends with whom you've been sharing this course, specifically to reflect on what you've learned.

Did a particular session resonate? Did it change how you think about writing? Did certain writing exercises stand out? How about your own story and characters, the ones you've created during the course? Do you think about them? Do they show up in your dreams? If so, those are the manuscripts begging to be told first.

And lastly, we hope you'll stay in touch. We'd love to hear your review of your experience with us. We'd love to get updates and find out how else we can help.

Please visit us at www.writeonproductions.com.

Consider signing up for Write On & Go, our subscription service (Think: a monthly digital gift box) stuffed with our own short videos of craft demos, prompts & exercises, and extra motivation, as well as virtual opportunities to interact with us and other experts directly.

And while you're at our site, join our free mailing list for more tips and tricks, resources, and NEWS that we're sure will help take your kidlit journey even farther.

That's it... For NOW!

Victoria & Cheryl

About the Authors

PHOTO CREDIT: KAREN WONG

Victoria J. Coe is the author of numerous books for children, including the uber-popular *Fenway and Hattie* series from Putnam Young Readers. A sought-after workshop presenter on POV and perspective, she created and taught a highly-regarded writing course at the Cambridge Center in Harvard Square for 3 years, where she first became known for the practical "Tips and Tricks" that she now regularly shares on social media. She lives with her husband in Boston & Duxbury, MA. Visit her at victoriajcoe.com or online @victoriajcoe.

Cheryl Lawton Malone earned her MFA in Creative Writing for Young People from Lesley University, and went on to author acclaimed picture books, including *Dario and the Whale* from Albert Whitman & Co. A former teacher of Writing for Children on the college and continuing education level, Cheryl is an in-demand manuscript consultant at Grub Street Boston. She and her husband live in Newton & Martha's Vineyard, MA. Connect with her at cheryllawtonmalone.com or on twitter @MaloneLawton or Facebook.

PHOTO CREDIT: KATHY TARANTOLA

www.ingramcontent.com/pod-product-compliance
Lightning Source LLC
Chambersburg PA
CBHW082110120626
46553CB00011B/3615